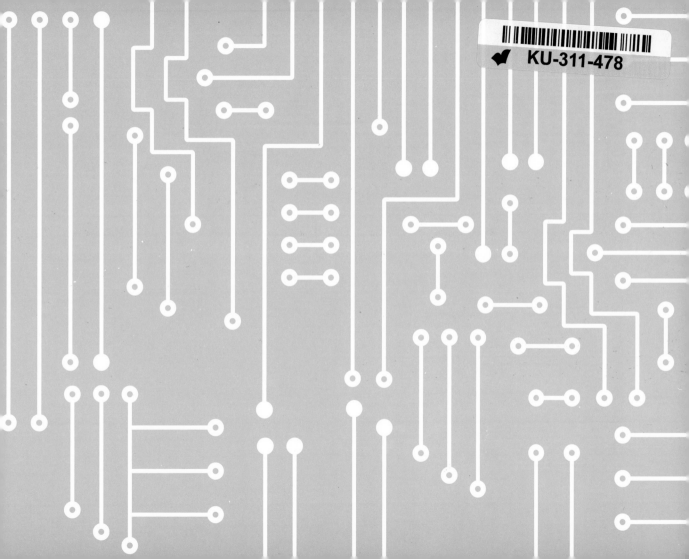
KU-311-478

First published in the United Kingdom in 2017 by
Pavilion Children's Books
43 Great Ormond Street
London
WC1N 3HZ

An imprint of Pavilion Books Company Ltd

ISBN 978-1-84365-323-3

A CIP catalogue record for this book is available from the British Library.

10 9 8 7 6 5 4 3 2 1

Reproduction by Mission Productions Ltd, Hong Kong
Printed and bound by Leo Paper Products Ltd, China

This book can be ordered direct from the publisher at www.pavilionbooks.com

Contents

Hello,
world!

Welcome to *Cool Coding*

I learned to program in an old bomb shelter. The school had built it during the Second World War, but by the time I arrived it had been turned into the Computer Club. We all wanted to play games on the computers, so I got my first taste of programming copying code from computing magazines line by line. At first I didn't know how the programs I was copying worked, but then I began to experiment and to write my own. Soon I was hooked.

Coding is logical, like a puzzle, but one with lots of possible solutions so you never get too stuck. Coding is creative: you can make games and tools and apps that you can share with friends and family. Coding doesn't need lots of equipment, doesn't make a mess, and can be something you do on a rainy day, or before it's time to go to bed. Boys and girls, young kids and retirees, people all over the world write code and share it with one another.

I still love coding today. It's my job now, and it's still my hobby, and with this book I hope I can get you excited about it too. Not only will the book teach you about the fundamental concepts of programming, but it'll tell you about useful tools and techniques, about how computers were used in the past and what they'll be able to do in the future, and it'll hopefully inspire you to go and write some code of your own!

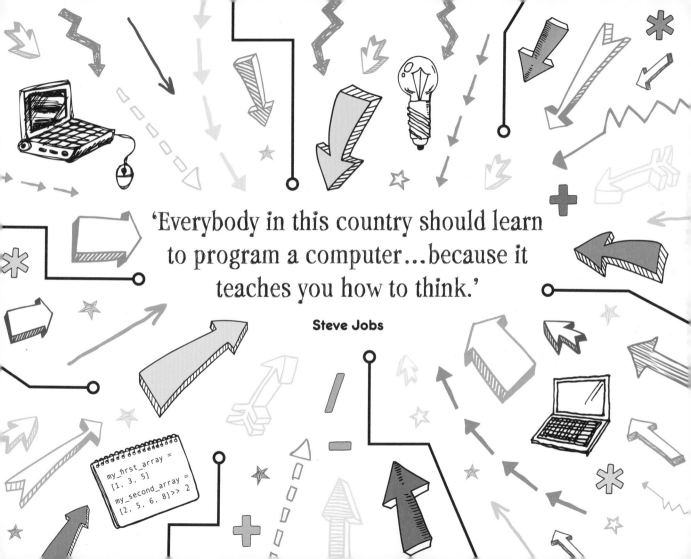

'Everybody in this country should learn to program a computer…because it teaches you how to think.'

Steve Jobs

```
my_first_array =
[1, 3, 5]
my_second_array =
[2, 5, 6, 8]>> 2
```

What Is a Program?

A computer that doesn't know what to do is just a very expensive paperweight. A program is what makes the computer play games, make music and draw images. A program tells the computer what to do.

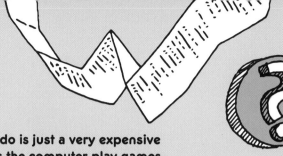

Following instructions

A program is like the list of instructions for assembling a heap of plastic toy bricks into a castle: a set of individual directives for the computer to carry out. Each individual instruction is only a very small step, like connecting two bricks together, but by the time the program is complete amazing things can be accomplished.

Just like a list of instructions, a program is read from top to bottom. Each line in the program is a statement, giving the computer an action to carry out. When that action is complete the computer will go on to the next line in the program, and so on until it reaches the end, when it will stop. A computer won't get bored or lose its place:

it'll keep following the program no matter how long it takes (though computers carry out instructions really quickly!).

Our first program

Computer programs are also called code, and a person who writes a computer program is called a coder or a programmer. That can be a person's job, but lots of people write programs for fun, including kids! Once you've written a program you can tell the computer to run it; that means the computer will follow the instructions and carry out the actions.

Let's see a program now:

```
print("I just started my first program!")
print("I just finished my first program!")
```

That's neat!
You can try out most of the coding examples in this book at the website jsfiddle.net (see page 108), but you will need to change the *print* command to *alert* to make them work.

The *print* instruction tells the computer to print out the line of text to the screen. When the code above is run the computer will first print out:

I just started my first program!

. . . and then:

I just finished my first program!

. . . as the computer follows the instruction on the first line and then the second. And – just like that – you've written a program!

Let's get started!
Just as people all over the world speak lots of different human languages, there are lots of different programming languages computer programs can be written in. Some languages are better for certain types of program than others, and some are more complicated than others. But no matter the language, the building blocks of all computer languages are the same.

This book will tell you all about coding, so when you try it for yourself you'll understand those building blocks, no matter what language you choose!

Colossus: The First Computer

These days, computers are everywhere, but until the 1940s a 'computer' was a *person* who did sums (computations) for a living, not a machine. It was boring work and impossible to do without making mistakes, so engineers looked for ways to build machines to do the job instead.

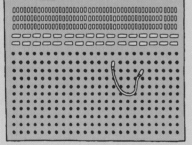

Enigma

During the Second World War armies on both sides sent instructions and reports back and forth via radio, and to stop the other side understanding them they encrypted their messages with codes. Britain assembled a team at Bletchley Park in Buckinghamshire to break the German codes, recruiting men and women who were good at maths, chess and crosswords. By 1941, with the help of Polish codebreakers and mechanical calculating machines designed by Alan Turing and others, they could read messages encrypted by the German's main code machine: Enigma.

That's neat!

Colossus was so secret that after the war only a few of the computers were kept; the rest were destroyed along with all the records. Everyone who knew about them was sworn to secrecy. So for a long time ENIAC, a machine built in 1946 in America, was thought to be the first computer. It wasn't until the mid-1970s that information about Colossus was made public. In 2007 a working replica of a Colossus Mark 2 was built and can be seen operating in the National Museum of Computing at Bletchley Park.

Colossus

But the German High Command used their own code system: Lorenz, a cipher too complex for even Turing's machines to crack. Something else was needed. Before the war Turing had speculated about building a machine that could solve any kind of mathematical problem. Now Tommy Flowers and Max Newman built just such a machine. It was named Colossus and it used electricity and vacuum tubes to perform

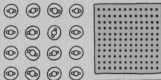

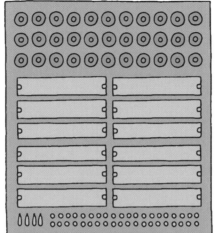

calculations. Unlike any previous machine it was electronic and programmable, so it could be set to solve any mathematical problem. It was the first computer!

Colossus Mark I was finished in December 1943 and could read coded messages at 1,000 characters per second from a paper tape. Mark 2, completed in June 1944, was five times faster. With this new device Bletchley Park could finally

crack the Lorenz code and read Hitler's messages to his commanders. The codebreaking efforts at Bletchley Park are thought to have shortened the war by years and saved millions of lives!

Words and Numbers

A computer program that couldn't remember anything wouldn't be very useful, so even the earliest computers had memory. A computer program remembers a piece of information by storing it in a variable.

When you define (use) a variable for the first time you need to give it a name. Then when you refer to that name later in the program you can get at the value inside it, or change it to something else. You set the value of a variable using the = sign, with the variable name on the left and the value you want to give it on the right:

> create a variable and give it the value '3'

> this will print out the value '3'

> change the value inside the variable to '5'

> now this will print the value '5'

```
my_first_variable = 3
print(my_first_variable)
my_first_variable = 5
print(my_first_variable)
```

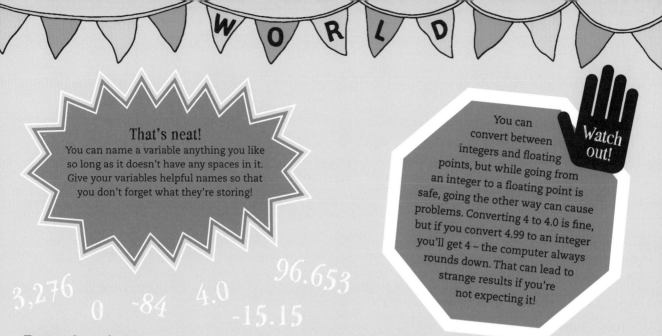

That's neat!
You can name a variable anything you like so long as it doesn't have any spaces in it. Give your variables helpful names so that you don't forget what they're storing!

Watch out!
You can convert between integers and floating points, but while going from an integer to a floating point is safe, going the other way can cause problems. Converting 4 to 4.0 is fine, but if you convert 4.99 to an integer you'll get 4 – the computer always rounds down. That can lead to strange results if you're not expecting it!

3,276   0   -84   4.0   96.653   -15.15

Types of numbers

Computers actually split numbers up into two types: integers and floating points. Integers are round numbers with no decimal places: 5, 7983, -6 and 0 are all integers. Floating point numbers are numbers with a decimal place, such as 1.29, -98.5 and 0.00002. Not every programming language worries about the difference, but a lot do. If you need to distinguish, 4 means the number is an integer, while 4.0 means it's a floating point.

Words

As well as numbers you can store words and even sentences in variables too! An individual letter is called a character, while a word or sentence is called a string (because it's made up of a *string* of individual characters). A single variable can contain an individual character or it can contain a whole string. A string can be as long as you want – you can store an entire book in a variable if you want to! Whenever you use a string it needs to be enclosed in quote marks, "like this".

Operators

Storing values in variables is all well and good, but computers come into their own when it comes to changing and combining those values. Computers were invented for number-crunching, and they're very good at it!

To manipulate variables, you use operators. This is really just a fancy programming term for plus, minus, divide and multiply, as well as a few others. Plus and minus are written + and - as normal, but multiply is written as * (not ×) and divide is / (not ÷).

However, as well as just adding numbers together and storing them in a variable you can add variables together too. Any place you might use a number on the right-hand side of the equals sign you can put in a variable instead:

Watch out!

Be very careful when dividing integers, since the result will be an integer too. So *var*/2 when *var* is 5.0 (a floating point) gives 2.5, but when *var* is 5 (an integer) it gives 2, since it rounds down to the nearest whole number. When dividing integers it's safest to convert to floating point first.

variable1 will equal 7

```
variable1 = 2 + 5

variable2 = 11 - variable1

variable3 = variable1 * variable2
```

variable2 will equal $11 - 7 = 4$

variable3 will equal $7 × 4 = 28$

Operators on assignment

You can assign variables back to themselves as part of an operation. For instance, to subtract 2 from a variable you can do *my_variable = my_variable – 2*.

This is so common that there are a set of assignment operators that let you do it really easily: +=, -=, *= and /=. They're a shorthand way of saying 'I want to do this to my variable'. So to divide *var* by 3 you can just write *var /= 3*.

To save even more time there's an even shorter way to add or subtract one from a variable: ++ and --. To add 1 to *var* you just need to write *var++*.

That's neat!

While operators are mostly used on variables that contain numbers, many programming languages will let you join two strings by 'adding' them together. They'll also let you add more text to the end of an existing string variable using the += operator. You can't subtract, divide or multiply strings, though, just numbers!

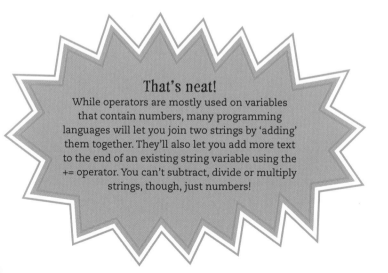

The remaining operator

There's one more operator available: %, which means modulus, and works like the remainder in long division. It doesn't get used very often, though, so don't worry about it.

Squashing Bugs

Computers are dumb. That doesn't mean they're bad at maths (they're incredibly good at it, in fact), but it does mean they will follow whatever instructions they are given to the letter, even if those instructions don't make sense.

A mistake in a computer program is called a bug. The story goes that one of the first computers kept producing the wrong answer until the operators took it apart and found a moth caught in the machinery – hence the name! These days, computers are moth-proof, and when they go wrong it's because there's a mistake in how they've been programmed.

Initially you might feel bad about having a bug in your code, but don't worry, even professional programmers spend lots of their time finding and fixing bugs in the code they've written!

Dealing with errors

Some bugs the computer will tell you about as soon as you try to run the program. For instance, syntax errors are mistakes like writing ?= rather than /=. The computer doesn't understand what that means and it will give you an error message, telling you what went wrong and where. Even if you don't understand the error message, go and look at that line of code and you'll often spot the problem right away.

Another kind of bug is a runtime error. That's when the computer understands your syntax, but at some point reaches an instruction it can't follow, such as trying to divide a number by 0. At this point the program will crash and print an error message.

Tracking down bugs

The worst bugs are when your program runs, but acts unexpectedly! In that case you're going to have to go through your code and figure out why it's not behaving. One trick is to add some *print()* commands to print out the value of important variables at various points in your program. By doing so you can track down the point when they stop having the values you expect. There are tools called debuggers that can do this sort of thing automatically, though they can be tricky to configure.

That's neat!

Sometimes you'll not be able to figure out the error. If there's no one you can ask, the best thing to do is to copy the type of error from the error message into a search bar. You'll almost always find lots of web pages explaining what it means. Professional programmers resort to this all the time when they get stuck!

Being Logical

Logic isn't just something Sherlock Holmes thinks about; your computer cares about it too.

Operating with logic

Logic has its own type of variable. As well as numbers and strings, you can have a Boolean. A Boolean can have one of just two possible values: **True** or **False**. Booleans are the simplest type of variable it's possible to have.

Where things get interesting is when you combine Booleans together to create new ones. Rather than adding, dividing or subtracting, Booleans have their own operators, called logical operators: **AND**, **OR** and **NOT**.

NOT (they are always written in caps) is the simplest: If b is equal to NOT a, then b is False if a is True, and vice versa. AND and OR are for when you combine more than one variable. If c is equal to a OR b then c is True if either of a or b is True (or if both are). If c is equal to a AND b then c is True only if both of a and b are True.

All of this is much easier to understand with truth tables, which say whether the result will be True or False for all the possible inputs:

NOT – b equals NOT a

a	b
True	False
False	True

OR – c equals a OR b

a	b	c
False	False	False
True	False	True
False	True	True
True	True	True

AND – c equals a AND b

a	b	c
False	False	False
True	False	False
False	True	False
True	True	True

To write them in code, the operators have symbols rather than names. NOT is **!**, OR is **||** while AND is **&&**.

Getting comparative

As well as setting a Boolean directly, you can set one by making a comparison. Comparisons are when you check whether some condition is True or False by comparing two values (or variables). There are a range of comparison operators available:

==	Equal to
!=	Not equal to
>	Greater than
<	Less than
>=	Greater than or equal to
<=	Less than or equal to

5 is not less than 3, so boolean2 will be False

Watch out!

Note that the *equal to* comparison operator is *two* equal signs, not one. If you forget one of them you can end up setting a variable to something rather than comparing it to something else. This is one of the most common mistakes in coding!

```
boolean1 = True

boolean2 = (5 < 3)

boolean3 = boolean1
&& boolean2

print (boolean3)

>> False
```

True AND False results in False

Who Codes?

When you think of a computer programmer, what sort of person pops into your mind? An adult or a child? A man or a woman? Someone who does it for their job, or someone who does it as a hobby? In fact, *anyone* can become a computer programmer: you can find coders of all ages, genders, nationalities and professions.

Coding as a job

There are lots of people for whom coding is a full-time job; they often have the job title 'computer programmer' or 'software engineer'. They aren't just making computer games and smartphone apps, though: computer programmers write the software that controls your washing machine, that transfers money from bank to bank, and that is inside a car. You might think that to become a professional computer programmer you need to go to university and take a Computer Science course, and that is one way. However, most full-time programmers didn't study programming at university. Many did other courses, often scientific, but not always. And many didn't go to university at all, getting into programming straight out of school, or starting with other jobs and moving into programming later.

Coding as a hobby

Coding isn't just something people do at work. Lots more people code in their spare time than do so for a living. They do it for fun, to learn, to make useful websites for friends or family, or to make games for other people to enjoy. Between the internet and smartphones it has never been easier for people to share their code with the world.

Many people start out learning to code as a hobby, but end up enjoying it enough they decide to turn it into a part-time or even full-time job. In fact, pretty much every professional coder learned most of their coding in their own time. App and website development are a great way for people to make some money working part-time, and to see how they enjoy coding professionally rather than just for fun.

Getting into coding

It's also never been easier to learn to code. There are lots of fantastic books out there about coding (like this one!), but you can also find everything you need to get started online. Pages 44 and 74 will get you started writing code, and page 108 has lots of links to websites that will lead on to more exciting and complicated projects.

Hello, World!

Computer programs, no matter how complicated, are really only useful if they have inputs (ways to control them) and outputs (ways to get information from them).

Writing things out

The simplest way for programs to communicate with us is by putting text on the screen. To do so you use something you'll have already seen in some of the examples earlier in the book: a *print* statement. It's very simple but it illustrates a lot of key concepts.

A statement is an instruction to the computer to do something. The *print* statement tells the program to display text on screen. You put the text you want to show in brackets after the *print* statement; this is called an argument, and it's used to tell a statement precisely what you want it to do. Put all that together and you can write whatever you want on screen:

> ## That's neat!
> It's a tradition in coding that the best way to show off a basic program in any programming language is to have it print out "Hello, world!". You'll run into it in lots of books and tutorials!

```
print("Hello, world!")
```

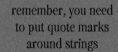

remember, you need to put quote marks around strings

Hello,
world!

Reading things in

Just as you can have a program write text out, you can have it read text in too! How precisely a program reads from the keyboard varies from language to language: you can read a single character (key press) at a time or a whole string until the user hits enter. Once you've done so, you can go ahead and store that input in a variable.

If you want your user to enter a number there's one more step. You see, to a computer the string "12" is different from the number 12; the first is a string just like "elephant" or "football", not a number it understands. To change from a string into a number you need to tell the program to convert it: a function like *int*("12") will convert it to the integer 12, while *float*("12") will turn it into the floating point number 12.0.

Punching In

In these days of touchscreens a keyboard may seem like a clunky way to write a program, but in the old days programs were stored and fed into computers using a far less convenient format: punched cards.

These were actual, physical cards with a series of holes punched in them. A computer read them by shining a light at the card and using a light sensor to determine if a particular hole had been punched or not, translating the cards into 1s and 0s.

Cards and computers

Punched cards actually predate the computer itself. They were first used way back in the early 1800s to control mechanical looms that wove patterns into cloth: the cards held the patterns to be woven. Back then there were no light sensors, so instead the cards were read by mechanical sensors that ran along the surface of the card. The cards had to be really thick and tough to survive being read this way!

Mechanical calculating machines in the 1800s and early 1900s used punched cards to store data and programs. Colossus, the first computer, read the messages it was working on from a paper tape with holes punched in it.

Working with holes

In the 1950s and 60s programmers would work out the program they wanted to run on paper, and then punch it into a series of cards using a keypunch, a device like a typewriter that would punch out holes in all the right places. One mistaken punch and the card would need to be thrown away. A complicated program could be hundreds or even *thousands* of cards arranged in precise order – woe betide anyone who knocked over one of these stacks!

As computers became more numerous and more powerful demand for punched cards rose too – by 1967 America alone was getting through two billion punched cards every year! But the taller and taller stacks of cards needed for more complex programs were becoming increasingly impractical, and by the 1970s a new technology, magnetic tape, began to replace the punched card as a way of inputting data to a computer.

In these days of flash drives and Wi-Fi it's amazing to think that people used to have to rely on stacks of cards to pass data to a computer!

Conditionals

Earlier you learned about Booleans, which are how computer programs keep track of whether things are True or False. Their real power, though, comes when you do different things based on those Boolean values. You can do that with conditionals.

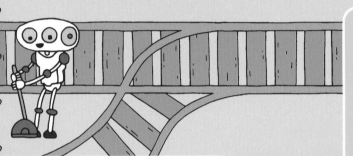

You can have an *if* statement on its own, but you can also pair it with an *else* statement. This doesn't need a condition, since it defines what to do if the conditional above turns out to be False. Again, you put the section of the code you want to run inside curly brackets. The reason for these brackets is that you can have lots of lines of code that are run inside these conditionals; the closing bracket says when that part of the code is done. This is called a block of code.

If or else

Conditionals are really simple. They're a way to tell the code to do one thing *if* something is True, *else* to do something different. To construct an *if* statement you put the condition (the thing you are checking) in brackets after the word 'if'. In most programming languages you then use curly brackets '{' and '}' to define what to do if that condition is True:

remember that double ==
means 'is equal to'

```
if(my_val==3)
{
 print("you entered the number three!")
}
```

Else and if

Along with *if* and *else* there is a third conditional statement: *else if* (*elif* in some programming languages). This is another *if* statement that only runs if the checks above it are False, and like *if* it requires a condition:

```
if(my_val==3)
{
 print("you entered exactly three")
}
else if (my_val<3)
{
 print("your number was less than three")
}
else
{
 print("to get here, your number must be more
than three")
 print("remember, you can have as much code as
you like inside a block!")
}
```

You can have lots of *else if* statements, one after another, if you like. The code will 'fall down' the set of conditional statements like a waterfall until it finds one that is True, at which point it will run the code inside that block.

That's neat!

You can put any code inside the block you put after a conditional statement, including more if statements! Having if statements inside if statements like this is called nesting.

Testing, Testing

We covered some of the mistakes it's possible to make while coding on page 16. In order to ensure your program does what you want it to do you need to test it.

Some techniques to effectively test your code are:

Test often Every time you make a small change, test your code. The smaller the code change, the easier it is to find and fix new bugs.

Try to break things Whenever you have an input, try deliberately entering incorrect values. Things that often cause problems include very long strings, empty strings ("") and negative numbers. These extreme inputs are called edge cases.

Use 'undo' When you've just added code that doesn't work it's often easier to use the undo function to step back to when it did work and then go forward line by line to find where the error came in.

Testing as a job

You might think that code developed by professionals would need less testing but that's not actually the case: no one writes bug-free code. Companies selling their software want to have as few bugs in the programs as possible. So some people in software development are full-time testers: rather than writing code they spend their time testing code other people have written. When they find a problem they file a bug report that lists how to trigger the bug and what the effect is. The programmers then use the report to find and fix the bug.

Code-testing code

Testing code is time-consuming and can be tedious, since you need to test the same thing over and over again to ensure it hasn't been broken by a later code change. So these days there is a move towards more and more automated testing.

Automated testing is essentially getting code to test itself. This involves writing more code that isn't part of your main program but is instead a test harness (so called because it goes around the main code). This harness runs your main program automatically, putting in various inputs and checking the outputs. These harnesses can be system tests, which go around the whole program, or unit tests, which go around individual parts of the code.

Writing these automated tests can seem like a waste of time compared to writing the program itself, but once you have them you'll know straight away any time you accidentally break something. That makes bugs very easy to find and fix, and can save you time in the long run!

Code for CPUs

There are a huge variety of programming languages out there, but one thing almost all of them have in common is that they are based on the English language. Even if you don't know a programming language you can usually look at some simple code in that language and work out roughly what it is doing.

Machine code

Computers, though, don't understand English. When they run a program they need it to be translated into machine code, instructions that their Central Processing Unit (CPU) understands. Machine code contains a very limited set of instructions that correspond to actual operations hardwired into the CPU.

The very first computers were programmed directly in machine code but this was extremely tricky work: programmers had to calculate a very precise set of values on every line to instruct the CPU what to do. Worse, every type of CPU had its own different machine code, so a program had to be rewritten from scratch to run on another type of computer.

Here's an example of some machine code:

```
77
29  20  b3
61  9e
70
0c  b7  f6
```

Assembly code

Assembly code was invented in the 1950s as a way to make programming somewhat simpler. Now the raw code was replaced by a set of short instructions that were (sort of) English, like *mov* for move, *jmp* for jump and *add* for, well, add. The language also included things like variable names to hold data. This assembly code could then be automatically turned into machine code for the CPU to run.

Here's an example of some assembly code:

```
loop:  add $t1,1
       bne $t1, $t2, end
       jmp loop
end:   nop
```

That's neat!

For a long time programmers still used assembly code if their program needed to be really small and fast, but as other programming languages have advanced, the machine code they automatically generate can often be better than even the best human-written assembly code. Now there are only a few niche cases where it still makes sense for people to write directly in assembly code.

Assembly code was easier to write than machine code, but it was still slow going, and different for each type of CPU. By the 1970s most programmers were using higher-level languages (so called because they were further 'up' from the CPU than low-level assembly language and machine code) that were more like English. These higher-level languages are then converted into machine code for the CPU to execute.

Code that Thinks

For as long as computers have existed, people have dreamed of them thinking for themselves. This is called Artificial Intelligence, or AI.

Crikey, he's good!

Computers playing chess

For a long time in Western culture the game of chess has been considered the pinnacle of cleverness: it's why movies and TV so often show smart people playing it. So early computer scientists spent a lot of time teaching computers to play chess. They felt that if they could do that, they could do anything.

However, it turns out that chess is actually far easier for a machine to master than something humans find trivial, like recognising a cat in a picture. In 1996 a supercomputer named Deep Blue beat Garry Kasparov, the world chess champion, but computers today are still less good at recognising cats than a three-year-old.

Beyond chess

Chess programs are an example of rules-based systems: humans understand how to play chess, so programmers write a bunch of rules for the program to follow. However, this approach doesn't work well for things we find it difficult to put into rules, such as identifying whether a picture has a cat in it. You can do it yourself easily, but can you break down precisely *how*, step by step?

Lots of recent research has gone into machine learning. Here we provide a framework for the computer to learn for itself, and then provide a large body of data for it to learn from (such as a lot of pictures, some with cats, some without). By running through all the data, the computer uses that framework to automatically build up a way to solve the problem. To do this we need clever frameworks like neural networks, and as much data as possible. Fortunately, the internet has an unlimited number of cat pictures!

Code that really thinks

The real dream of many computer scientists is a machine that is truly intelligent. Back in 1950, Alan Turing invented the Turing Test to determine if a computer really is intelligent. The test involves a person having a conversation with someone they can't see. If they think it's a person and it turns out to be a computer, then that computer can be considered to be intelligent. No computer program has managed to beat this test yet, but coders are trying to produce one that can. Can you imagine what the implications would be if they managed it? After all, such a program could be considered to be alive . . .

Dealing with Data

We've met variables, which let us store pieces of information, but what if we have a bunch of data, like the marks everyone in your class got on a test? Rather than creating lots of variables, we can create a single thing that can store lots of different values.

Some programming languages call these arrays, some call them lists. If a variable is like a box that you can keep a value in, then an array is like a chest of drawers, with each drawer able to store an individual value.

Creating arrays

To use arrays we need another kind of bracket – [ ]. These are called square brackets. When we create arrays, we put all the bits of data (which we call elements when they're in an array) inside these square brackets, separated by commas.

create an array containing three elements

```
my_first_array = [1, 3, 5]
```

Once you have data in an array you can read or change individual elements. To tell the program which element we want to access we give it an index, like a page number in a book. It's just the number of the element we want, counting from the beginning of the array.

Watch out!

Unlike humans, computers start counting at 0. So the index of the first element in the list is 0, the second element is 1 and so on. It's easy to forget this one, so don't feel bad if it trips you up occasionally.

Accessing data

To access a particular element, we use square brackets again, containing the index of the element we want. So x[0] means the first element in an array named x. If we just say x with no brackets, we're referring to the whole array.

```
my_second_array = [2, 5, 6, 8]
print(my_second_array[0])
>> 2
my_second_array[1] = 3
print(my_second_array)
>> [2, 3, 6, 8]
```

now just print out the first element – remember, array indexes start at 0!

let's change the second value (so index of 1)

and now let's print the whole array

You can do lots of neat things with an array, like check how many elements it has, rearrange the order, add elements to it or take them out. If you do take an element out then all the ones after it move up, like taking a carriage out of the middle of a train.

The world's first computer programmer...

Meet Ada. Ada Lovelace, born in 1815, was the world's first computer programmer. This would be impressive enough, but she lived at a time when women weren't expected to tackle anything much more complicated than embroidery. And to top it all off, she did all this a century before anyone actually built a computer...

Daughter of the famous (and scandalous) poet Lord Byron, Ada was taught maths and science in an attempt to keep her from following in her father's badly behaved footsteps, and she fell in love with the subjects. At 17 she met a man who would change her life: Charles Babbage.

The Difference Engine

Babbage was an engineer, astronomer and inventor. Being an astronomer back then involved doing a lot of sums, and Babbage wanted to make a machine to do them for him: a machine would never get bored and wouldn't make mistakes.

This was the 1820s, though. There were no computer chips, no transistors, not even any electricity. But that didn't stop Babbage. His machine would be made of nothing more than cogs, gears and other mechanisms. He named it the Difference Engine.

Babbage spent 20 years and huge sums of government money on the project, but the technology of the time just wasn't up to the challenge, and he could never get the machine to work.

When Ada met Charles, he told her about a new idea of his. It was an even more complicated machine, the Analytical Engine, which could do any sort of calculations. This was the first time anyone had thought of a computer. Ada was fascinated by the whole idea, and helped Babbage figure out how it could work. By doing so she

That's neat!
Ada never saw a real computer, but modern engineers have named a programming language, Ada, after her.

The Analytical Engine

became the first person to ever work out how to program a computer. The Analytical Engine was never made either, but that didn't stop Ada figuring out how to use it. And while Babbage was still thinking in terms of doing simple mathematics, she foresaw that one day computers would do amazing things, even composing music!

Making Things Functional

So far all the program examples you've seen have been of a single set of instructions, executed in order. However, all but the simplest programs rely on functions: blocks of code split out that can be called from other places in the program. Functions let you write code in manageable chunks, and save you from copy/pasting code if you need to do the same thing in different places.

Getting into a function

Function definitions often start with a keyword that varies from programming language to language, like *function* or *def*. Then your function needs a unique name (which, like a variable, can't contain any spaces). After the name comes a set of brackets that can contain a number of arguments. These are variables that are passed into your function that you can then use inside it. Finally, you add some curly brackets. These define the code block that gets run as part of the function.

You can call a function from anywhere in the code by writing the name of the function followed by a pair of brackets containing the same number of variables as in the function definition. You'll notice this looks like calling the *print* statement. That's because *print* is a function defined by the language itself, that works just like the ones you can define.

Variables declared in an argument or inside the code block are scoped to that block: they don't exist outside it. This means you don't need to worry about reusing variable names; so long as you don't reuse them within the same block you're fine.

Getting out of a function

Your code block can contain any code you like, plus a new, special statement: *return*. When the program reaches a *return* statement it immediately exits the function and jumps back to the line it was called from without executing the rest of the function code. If you just put *return* it will jump back on its own. If you put *return* and then a variable or value it will return with that value. If the code reaches the end of the function without hitting a return statement it will return without any value.

> defining a function with one argument

```
function calculate_square(my_var)
{
  result = my_var*my_var
  return result
}

var = calculate_square(3)
var = calculate_square(var)
print(var)
>> 81
```

> return the 'result' variable

> call the function passing in '3' as the argument

> call it again on the result

39

Coding Tools

In the end program code is just text, so you can write it in any text editor you like. However, over the years, developers have come up with a range of tools to make writing code easier.

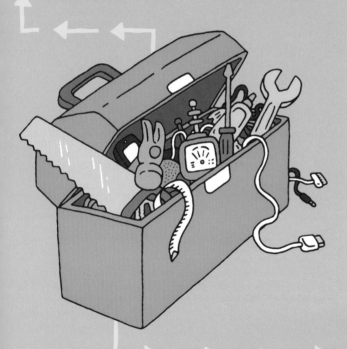

A smarter text editor

Some text editors are designed for writing code. One very useful trick they have is to change the text colour to separate out variables, statements and other things. They'll also make strings stand out, which is very handy when you forget the closing quote on a string and it ends up going on forever . . .

These editors need to understand the programming language you're using to do these tricks; most will support many common languages. Some can detect it automatically from what you write or from the extension of the filename (.py for Python, for example); others will have an option in the menu to set it.

These little tweaks may not sound like much but actually they make reading and writing code *far* easier – once you've tried it you'll never go back to a boring old black-and-white editor!

IDEs

An IDE, or integrated development environment, looks like a text editor on the surface but is much more powerful. As well as smart colour coding an IDE will have a *play* button to build and run your program directly, and will often be able to find and organise all your functions. They may even have more complex tools like debuggers built into them. IDEs are much more complex than a text editor and are not as straightforward to set up and start using. They also need to be configured for each language you are using, and some may only support one particular programming language.

While just about every programmer uses a smart text editor of some kind, not all use an IDE; you should start out with a text editor and then try an IDE later to see how useful you find it.

Coding in your browser

These days the internet has sites that will let you write, run and experiment with code for a number of different languages right in your browser. This is a fantastic way to jump straight in and start writing some simple programs without needing to install anything on your computer.

Going Loopy

Computers are great at doing things over and over again. If you wanted your program to do something repeatedly you could copy and paste the code lots of times, but that would take up lots of space.

A better approach is to put blocks of code (remember, a block is code surrounded by curly brackets) inside a structure called a loop, where they'll be run multiple times.

While loops

The simplest kind of loop is a *while* loop. It's called that because it continues to loop around executing the same code *while* some condition is True. Using it, you can write code that keeps running until something interesting happens.

```
print("Small numbers get
big fast when you double
them over and over")
x = 1
while (x<=1000000)
{
    x = x*2
    print(x)
}
print("Now x is over
1,000,000!")
```

this line is outside the loop, so it runs when the loop ends

make x twice as big as it was

keep looping until x is bigger than 1,000,000

For loops

Often you want to loop a fixed number of times and then move on; this type of loop is called a *for* loop. A *for* loop loops *for* a set number of times. For loops include an index – this keeps track of the number of times the program has been around the loop so far. Be careful, though – just like in arrays, the index starts at 0, not at 1!

The number of times the *for* loop runs can be a fixed number, like the example, or it can be an integer variable. Different programming languages write *for* loops in different ways, so you'll need to look up how to write them in your language.

the name of the index here is i, and you want to loop 10 times

```
print("Start the
countdown...")
for (i, 10)
{
    print(10 - i)
}
print("Blast off!")
```

i will go from 0 to 9, so this will count from 10 to 1

That's neat!
There are a couple of ways the code inside a loop can change things. A *continue* instruction tells the program to skip the rest of the lines and go back to the start of the loop for the next run, while a *break* instruction tells it to end the loop straight away.

Get Coding!

Now that you've learned some of the fundamentals of coding, it's time to try it for yourself! Rather than worry about all the writing, though, you're going to start out with Scratch, a really straightforward programming language that lets you drag and drop code into place. You can even do it on a tablet!

← → C https://scratch.mit.edu

Head to www.scratch.mit.edu and click (or tap) **Create**. That puts you in the coding area, where you can drag code segments from the menu on the left and join them to other segments to make a program. Try joining a few together now – you need to line up the little notches. You can pull them apart too, and drag them off the screen to discard them. Different pieces of code are available from different menus on the left – take a look at what's available.

All programs start with code from the **Events** section – you can tell these because the segments have a lump on top so nothing can go above them. Pick the one that has a flag on it. Connect segments under that, and then hit the flag button in the top left to run your program.

Blasting off

OK, let's code! To start with, create a program that counts down from 10 to 1 then says 'Blast off!', just like the mission controller for a rocket. Here are a few hints to get you started:

⚙ You're doing something (counting down) lots of times, so you need a *loop*.

⚙ You also need a *variable*, to keep track of what number you're on.

⚙ You'll need to print out the variable, then decrease it next time around the loop so you count down.

You can also look back at the example on page 43. However, this is in a different language, so you won't be able to copy it precisely! This shows how different languages do the same thing in slightly different ways. If you get really stuck, check out the answer at the bottom of this page.

Once you manage that, why not try making the character actually blast off into space once the countdown completes? **Hint** You'll need another loop, a *move* command and a *wait* command.

Bits and Bytes

If you were to take a very powerful microscope and examine the CPU of a computer, you wouldn't find numbers or words or any of the other values we move around in programs. Instead you would find millions of transistors. A transistor is really just an incredibly tiny on/off switch. When the transistor is on we give it the number 1, and when it is off we give it the number 0. In the end everything in a computer, no matter how complicated, comes down to 1s and 0s.

We call each of these values a single bit (short for binary digit). Each bit can be set to 1 or 0. It's the computer equivalent of an atom: deep down, everything in a computer is made of bits.

A bit more information

Rather than work with bits directly though, early computer systems collected them into groups of 8, which was the smallest number of bits that could be read or written at a time. One of these groups of 8 bits is called a byte, and has room to store a single character (like 'a' or '+').

But even a byte is a really tiny amount of information. These days we need much bigger numbers! A kilobyte (kB) is 1,000 bytes, while a megabyte (MB) is 1,000,000 bytes and a gigabyte (GB) is 1,000,000,000 bytes. There are bigger prefixes too: tera- means 12 zeroes, peta- 15 and exa- 18, but for a while at least those numbers are mostly the preserve of supercomputers!

Counting the bits we send

When we talk about how much data is being sent between computers we talk about the bit rate – the number of bits per second. Just like with bytes we can have kilobits per second, megabits and so on. To keep things straight, when coders abbreviate mega*bytes* they write MB (with a big B), but when they abbreviate mega*bits* they write Mb (with a small b).

Weirdly, the abbreviation of kilo- is a small k, while mega- and giga- are capital M and G respectively.

Watch out!

Oddly, sometimes a kilobyte means 1,000 bytes, and sometimes 1,024, while a megabyte can be 1024 × 1024 and so on. It's because sometimes, as we'll see on the next page, it's more convenient if things are a power of 2. The two are pretty close to each other, so normally we don't need to worry about which is being used.

Watch out!

bit	1
byte	8 bits
kilo-	1,000 bytes
mega-	1,000,000 bytes
giga-	1,000,000,000 bytes
tera-	1,000,000,000,000 bytes
peta-	1,000,000,000,000,000 bytes
exa-	1,000,000,000,000,000,000 bytes!

How Computers Count

As humans we count in decimal: that means we have ten types of numbers from 0 to 9, and we combine them to produce bigger numbers (like 42). Decimal is also called base 10. Humans use decimal because when we first learn to count we use our fingers to keep track of the numbers – we have ten fingers, so we use base 10!

Two by two

Computers don't have fingers, though. As we've just seen, computers really see everything as 0s and 1s. This means their way of counting only has two types of number: 0 and 1. This is base 2, better known as binary.

In binary, the two types of number get combined to make larger numbers. Just as decimal numbers go from 0 up to 9 and then go on to 10, 11 and 12, binary works the same way, only much faster: 1, then 10, then 11, then 100 and so on. This can end up getting pretty unwieldy – 86 in binary is 1010110, for instance.

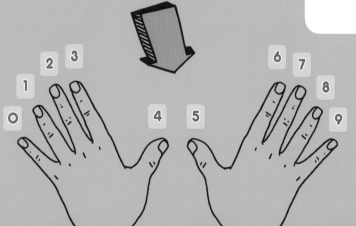

That's neat!
Now that you understand binary you'll be able to get an old programming joke: 'There are only 10 types of people in the world: those who understand binary, and those who don't.'

Sixteen by sixteen

So programmers actually more often use a third type of numbering: hex (short for hexadecimal), which is base 16. The reason this is useful is that 16 is a power of 2: 16 is 2×2×2×2. That makes it very easy to convert from binary to hex and back, and it means a byte (which is 8 bits, so 8 binary digits) fits into two hex digits.

Base 16 means that hex has 16 types of numbers. Since our normal numbers don't go up that high, hex uses letters to fill in the rest. Hex goes from 0 to 9 just like decimal, but then goes A, B, C, D, E and F. That means that 30 in decimal is 1E in hex (1 × 16 + 14), and with just two hex digits you can count up to 255 (which is FF in hex and 11111111 in binary).

Can you work out what the following hex numbers are in decimal?

a. 1C
b. 31
c. A8

Numberline

decimal	binary	hex	decimal	binary	hex	decimal	binary	hex
1	1	1	7	111	7	13	1101	D
2	10	2	8	1000	8	14	1110	E
3	11	3	9	1001	9	15	1111	F
4	100	4	10	1010	A	16	10000	10
5	101	5	11	1011	B			
6	110	6	12	1100	C			

Answers a) 28, b) 49, c) 168

49

Keeping Things Tidy

When you start writing a program it's usually pretty easy to keep the whole thing in your head. But once it gets longer, or if you take a break and then come back to it, you may not remember why you did things a particular way. Keeping your code neat will make it a lot easier to work with. Here are a few tricks you can use.

Helpful names

Rather than use cryptic, short variable or function names, use plain, descriptive names. If you have a variable that stores the number of cats a person has, name it *number_of_cats* rather than *c* or *noc*. And don't reuse variables to store completely unrelated values later in the program (like reusing *number_of_cats* to store the room temperature), just create a new one – variables are free!

Short lines

Try and keep your lines of code short enough that they always fit on your screen. That way you don't end up having to scroll back and forth, and each line will be short enough that you can easily figure out what it does.

camelCase and snake_case

Variables and function names can't have spaces in, but programmers have come up with ways to still use multiple words in their names.

One is to run all the words together and capitalise all the first letters after the initial one: *justLikeThis*. That's called camel case, because the capital letters make it look a bit like the humps on a camel. The other way is to keep everything lower case but replace the spaces with '_': *just_like_this*. That's called snake case, because the names end up long and thin, like a snake.

hi_there_humpy

Some programmers prefer camel case, some prefer snake case; you can use whichever you prefer. Whichever you do use, be consistent within a program, or else things will start looking messy.

HiThereLimbless

⫽ Comments

You can include comments in code. Comments are messages that you can use to remind yourself or anyone else who reads the code about what a function is doing or what's happening in a particular place. Their syntax varies, but starting with '//' is a common way to write them. In this book we've replaced traditional comments with graphics boxes to make them easier to follow, but a typical example (from page 22) would be:

```
print("Hello, world!") //
remember, you need to put
quote marks around strings
```

You can end up overusing comments – don't use them when the code is already obvious. A good rule of thumb is to write a comment to explain what each function is meant to do, and also any time you write a particularly complicated piece of code.

Inside Your Computer

PCs, laptops, smartphones and tablets may all look different, but inside they have the same core components.

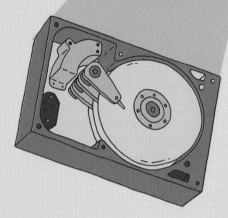

CPU

The CPU, or Central Processing Unit, is the computer's brain. It's the part of the computer that executes the programs, reading the machine code, doing all the calculations, and carrying out the instructions. Modern CPUs are chips of silicon about the size of a fingernail, but that tiny chip contains *billions* of transistors, each so small they're only a few dozen atoms wide. Packing in all those transistors means that CPUs can get very hot when they run, so larger, more powerful devices include a fan to keep them cool.

Storage

This is the part of the system used to store data; not just the programs themselves but photographs, movies, music and other files. Storage doesn't depend on batteries or power – your computer won't forget things in storage even when it shuts down. Until recently computer storage was mostly in the form of hard drives, which used a stack of thin metal platters to store data magnetically. Now more and more systems (particularly smaller ones like phones) have moved to solid-state storage, which stores data on computer chips called flash memory.

Memory

Your computer can fit lots of things in its storage, but can only read and write to it fairly slowly (compared to how quickly the CPU can do things, that is). To speed things up the computer has another kind of fast storage called the memory or RAM (short for Random Access Memory). The computer's RAM is much faster than its storage, and it's where programs and other files are kept while they're being used. It's more expensive than storage, though, so you'll have less space in memory than in storage. It's also volatile, which means that it needs constant power to remember things – when you switch the computer off it forgets everything in its memory.

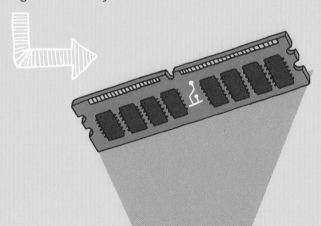

Input/Output

Along with those core internals, computers also have input devices, like mice, keyboards, and touchscreens, which allow you to communicate with them, and output devices, like displays and speakers, that let the computer communicate with you. Since these are often not built directly into the machine most computers have ports that let you plug them in. External devices like mice and speakers that connect to the computer are called peripherals.

User Interfaces

So far we've looked at interacting with a program through lines of text; this is the simplest method to use. Programmers call this a command line interface, or CLI. Most computer users have trouble using a CLI. However, there's another way.

Getting graphical

That other way is a graphical user interface, or GUI. A GUI lets your program show your users pictures, menus and other elements, and lets them interact with it using a mouse or touchscreen. GUIs take more work to create, so they're not something you should worry about until you've mastered the basics of programming, but they're very user-friendly.

To create a GUI you need a GUI framework. Each programming language has a different set of frameworks with different ways of doing things, all designed to help coders create a GUI for their program. Some languages come with a GUI framework built in, and that's usually the best to start with, but there will be numerous others you can download and use.

Elements of interaction

All GUI frameworks revolve around a set of key elements you'll recognise from computer programs you've used:

Text boxes display text to users or allow them to enter text themselves.

Buttons are things users click to tell the program to do something.

Dropdowns are a list of options the users can pick from.

GUI frameworks will let you write code to define elements like buttons, along with their position, size and other properties. They often also include a GUI designer, which will let you draw out your GUI visually, and then generate part of the code for you. While it's best to start out creating a few buttons in code to understand how they work, designers are much quicker to use.

That's neat!

The way elements like buttons work is with a special type of function named a *callback*. A *callback* is just a normal function, but its name is passed into another function, which will then call back to it when a condition is met. So when a button is pressed, that *callback* function gets run.

Check boxes are options your users can toggle on or off.

Radio buttons are like check boxes, but users can only pick one option.

Labels help describe what all the other elements are for.

Sliders let users scroll when not everything can be fitted on screen.

Feeling Classy

All the programming we've seen so far has been examples of procedural programming, using independent variables and functions. However, since the 1970s another style of coding has become increasingly popular: object-oriented programming, which revolves around classes.

Class is in session

A class is a way to store functions and variables within objects where they naturally belong, rather than having them spread out all over the place. For instance, if you wanted to write a program about dogs you could create a *dog()* class. Then you would make any variables or functions that related to dogs part of that *dog()* class.

Like a function, a class needs to be defined before it is used. This definition involves curly brackets like a function – the functions and variables are then put inside this block to show they belong to the class. In some languages functions inside a class are called methods.

Not only is this a nice, logical way to group variables and functions, but it means every time you want to consider a dog in your program

Right, let's classify this stuff!

you just need to instantiate the *dog()* class. Instantiate just means assigning it to a variable, just as you do with a string or an integer. You can then access any of the functions or variables in the class with a dot operator, '.'. Functions can also access internal variables by referring to *this* or *self* (depending on the language).

```
class dog()
{
  name = "unknown"
  function speak()

  {
   print("Woof! My name is "+this.name)
  }
}

my_dog = dog()
my_dog.name = "Rex"
my_dog.speak()
```

- defining the dog() class
- this variable is part of the dog() class
- this function is part of the dog() class
- uses the internal 'name' variable
- instantiate a variable of type 'dog()'
- set the 'name' variable for my_dog
- will print "Woof! My name is Rex"

Under construction

The example above does have one problem – you have to set the *name* variable before you call *speak()* or you won't get a sensible result. It's quite often the case that some variables in a class need to be set before it can be used, and object-oriented programming solves this with a constructor. This is a special function in the class that is always called when you instantiate it (e.g. assign it to a variable). In our example above you could change the class definition to include a constructor that sets the *name* variable. Then you could write code like this:

- another_dog.name will be filled in immediately

```
another_dog = dog("Spot")

another_dog.speak()
```

- will print "Woof! My name is Spot"

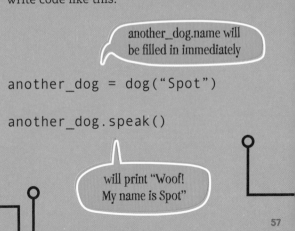

Inheritance

As we've just seen, classes are a great way to store and reuse functions and variables associated with something. Even better, though, another feature of classes lets you minimise the need to rewrite code and keep things logical: inheritance.

Meet the children

Inheritance, or subtyping, is when you define new child classes (or subclasses) that inherit from a parent class (or superclass). These child classes still retain all of the functions and variables of their parent class, but can also have their own variables and functions specific to them.

For instance, once you have defined a *dog()* class you could define child classes for specific breeds of dog. Anything that is common to all dogs goes into the parent *dog()* class, while anything specific to the breed goes into the individual child classes. Each child class is its own breed of dog with its own characteristics (colour, etc.), but also has all the properties of the parent class, which are common to all dogs (having four feet, etc.).

```
class husky() inherits from dog()
{
  function howl()
  {
    print("Awoo!")
  }
}

my_dog = husky()
my_dog.howl()
my_dog.name = "Blue"
```

each language has its own syntax for inheritance

instantiate a variable of type 'husky()'

can access variables and functions defined in the child class

can access variables and functions from the parent class

Morphing around

Not only is this a great way to avoid needing to duplicate code in the child classes, but it lets you be really flexible with functions too. Any time you have a function that expects a class as one of its arguments you can use a child class of that parent instead – that's because (to use our example above) an instance of the *husky()* class is an instance of the *dog()* class too. This is called polymorphism.

By default, a child class inherits all variables and functions a parent has. Child classes can also change the parent class behaviour by overriding it. To do this, just define a function in the child class with the same signature (name and arguments) as the parent, and the version defined in the child will override that of the parent. That means whenever that function gets called, the version defined in the child class gets used instead of the one from the parent class.

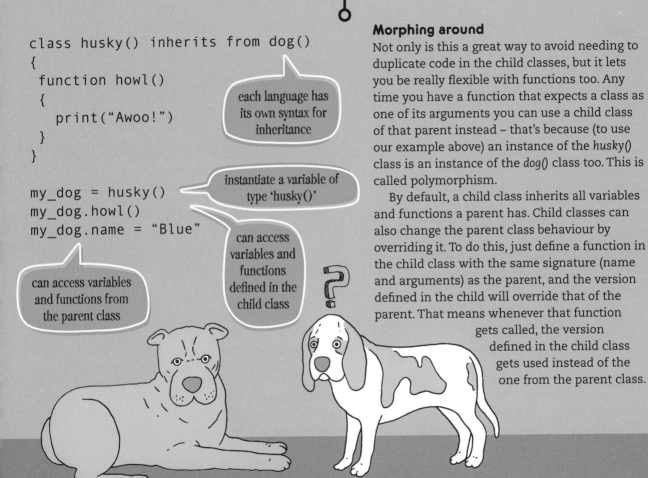

Getting Out There

While to begin with you may be writing programs to learn about coding or for your own amusement, the best part of programming is when you share your programs with other people.

For short, straightforward programs it makes sense to finish them and then let others have a go. But for large and complicated programs it often makes sense to share them with other people while you are still working on them – the feedback people give you can be invaluable.

Alpha and beta

Once you have a program at a stage where some of it works, but before you've finished all of it, you may want to share it with your friends and family, so they can tell you what they think so far. In software programming this is called an alpha release.

Ask them to tell you what they like about it and what they think could be better. By asking now, you might find you want to make changes to how your program works – better now than after you've written the whole thing!

A beta release is when you think the program is done, but before you've necessarily ironed out every bug. Again, share it with friends and family, but now ask them to deliberately go through and see if they can find ways to break the program. This break-fix cycle is called beta testing (and the people you give it to are called beta testers).

The idea of a beta is to make sure the program works precisely the way you want it to and that your users won't have any issues with it.

Birdhouse 0.3

Birdhouse 0.9

Birdhouse 1.0

That's more like it!

Versioning

Version numbers are a way to keep track of all the different versions of a program you give out – the newer the version, the higher the number. Traditionally, pre-release (alpha and beta) versions of a program are given versions of the form 0.x, so 0.1, 0.2, 0.14. Each new version increases the number on the right side of the dot by one.

The first release version of a program is 1.0 – the '1' shows it's ready for release. If you keep producing versions after that, adding features or fixing bugs, then you once again increment the number on the right of the dot: 1.1, 1.7, 1.16. If you ever make some really big changes you can call the new version 2.0 to show it's a completely new version of your program.

Beyond the Code

There's more to coding than just writing code. You see, it doesn't matter if you have created the most fantastic program in the world if no one can figure out how to use it. That's where documentation and support comes in.

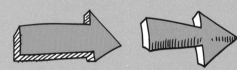

Documentary evidence

Documentation is the words, pictures and sometimes videos that explain how to use your program. In the old days programs would come in a big cardboard box, because along with the program itself (on CD or floppy disk) would be a hefty printed manual that would contain all the instructions.

Now, though, documentation is much more likely to be found on the internet. Ideally you should have documentation that tells people how to install your program and all the things they can do with it. Writing documentation can take quite a bit of time and often isn't as much fun as writing the program itself, but it's vital if you plan to give the program to people who won't be able to ask you things in person. You may also find writing the documentation helps improve your program: if you find yourself having trouble explaining how to do something, maybe your program needs changing . . .

Often the best place to put documentation on how to use your program is into the program itself. Some programs come with tutorials that walk a user step-by-step through certain tasks to introduce them to all the basics. Many also have help screens, pages that pop up when the user presses a '?' icon – that screen can then tell them about that part of the program.

If you find people keep asking you the same questions about your program you can put

together an FAQ (short for Frequently Asked Questions). This is a documentation page in the form of a series of questions with answers for each – that way it's easy for people to find the answers to common questions they might have.

A supporting role

Professional software companies have support staff, people whose job it is to help users understand their programs and use them as well as possible. This is one way companies can give away their programs but still make enough money to stay in business – other companies that find their software really useful pay for support to get the most out of the programs, and to deal with any problems they run into.

Not My Type

So far we've mentioned in passing that there are lots of different programming languages. Just like human languages, they can all express the same thing, but they do so in ways that can be very different. Some programming languages are broadly similar, like Spanish and Italian, while some have fundamentally different approaches, like English and Cantonese.

Static vs dynamic typing

One fundamental difference between categories of languages revolves around how they treat types. Types refer to the contents of a variable: integers, strings, a user-defined class and so on. Some languages are statically typed – that means that a variable must always contain the same type, often defined when the variable is created. In contrast a dynamically typed language means that any variable can contain any type at any time, and it can change at any time throughout the program.

Dynamically typed languages are generally quicker to write and more flexible, since you don't need to tell the program what variable you're planning to use, or worry about putting the wrong type into a variable. The code also ends up being more concise without all the type declarations.

The big advantage of statically typed languages is that because the system always knows what type everything is, it can catch any type-based mistakes (like trying to add a string and a number together) as soon as you run it, whereas dynamically typed languages will only fail when they reach that part of the program.

That's neat!

Dynamically typed languages will sometimes need to check whether a particular variable is of the type needed. Rather than check the type itself, it can often be better to just check whether the thing you want to do to it (like add it to another number) is valid or not. This technique is called duck typing, from the expression…

'If it walks like a duck and quacks like a duck, it's a duck.'

Yep, I'm a duck

Linguistic differences

Generally speaking, concise, flexible languages that use techniques like dynamic typing are considered higher level than slower to write, more static languages. This means they are further removed from the machine code that the computer actually runs. Over time more and more programmers have moved to higher level languages, as they can get more done with less code and time.

It's worth trying out multiple programming languages – different languages are better suited to different tasks. By learning new languages you'll also be exposed to new techniques that you can apply to *all* your programming.

Picture It

While old computers focused on text on a screen, computers nowadays can produce astonishing graphics – just about every animated movie and TV show, whether it's in 2D or 3D, is now produced primarily on computers.

If you want to produce graphics in your program you'll need a graphics library. Some languages have a built-in library, or you can download a wide array of other libraries for each language. If there is a built-in library these are usually the best way to get started; they may not be the most powerful or specialised, but they're usually straightforward to use and there will be lots of help online.

Two dimensions
A 2D graphics library will let you draw shapes (not just triangles, circles and rectangles, but more complex shapes like polygons) and choose their colour and outline.

It will also let you add text and pictures that you've downloaded from the internet.

To make graphics that move, your program will need to draw lots and lots of individual frames of animation, quickly enough that the human eye can't distinguish the individual drawings. Your graphics library should have a range of functions to make this much easier than coding each frame by hand.

Three dimensions

Some graphics libraries only produce 2D graphics, but others can do 3D as well. These involve creating scenes out of objects.

Producing 3D graphics can be pretty complicated; it's worth giving 2D graphics a try first. Game engines often contain some of the easiest 3D graphics engines to use.

Objects can be primitives like cubes and cones, or models of more complex objects that are provided by the library or downloaded. These objects are then textured to choose their colour, and then the system renders them into a 2D image based on where a virtual camera is pointing.

That's neat!

Along with primitives like cones, spheres and rectangles, many 3D graphics libraries include... a teapot. It's because one of the pioneers of 3D graphics needed a model for some testing. Since they were having tea at the time they carefully measured their teapot and used that, sharing it with other people online. It's also become an in-joke for animators to hide that teapot in the background of 3D movies!

Going Somewhere?

While we've explored all sorts of programming concepts like loops, conditionals and functions, there's one fundamental programming concept we haven't tackled yet: the *goto* statement.

▷ ◦ ◦ ◦ ◦ ◦ ▷ ◦ ◦ ◦ ◦ ◦ ▷ ◦ ◦ ◦ ◦ ◦ ▷ ◦ ◦ ◦ ◦ ◦ ▷ ◦ ◦ ◦ ◦ ◦ ▷

To goto or not to goto?

A *goto* statement is made up of two parts, a label somewhere in the code, and a *goto* that tells the code to 'go to' that label. When the code reaches the *goto* it jumps to the label and carries on from there.

```
[lbl] my_label
print("I will say this forever!")
goto my_label
```

define a label

now jump back to the label

Watch out though – there are very good reasons why you should never use *goto*. The problem is that while it's easy to add a *goto* to your code, the more of them there are, the harder it is to follow the path the program will take through the code. After a while your program will turn into a mess of spaghetti code that is very hard to debug.

So while almost all programming languages still include the *goto* statement, since the 1960s programmers have been urged to avoid it. In programming, functionality that is available but shouldn't be used is called deprecated – it means there are now better ways to deal with this, in this case functions and loops.

Smelly code

Along with spaghetti code there are other things that can make code difficult to read and debug. These include:

- Lots of copy/pasted code that is very similar.
- Very long functions that take up multiple screens.
- Very long individual lines of code.
- Functions that takes lots of arguments.

Programmers refer to these as 'bad smells' – they are signs that the code may work, but it will be difficult to change without accidentally breaking something, and when it breaks it will be hard to fix.

Don't worry if your code has one or more of the above; programs that change over time often end up like this. The solution is refactoring, which is like spring-cleaning for code. It's the process of changing the code, not to make it do new things, but to be more manageable while doing the same thing. This usually involves turning duplicated code into a single function that can be called from multiple places, breaking up overlong lines and functions into separate chunks, and replacing *goto* statements with functions and loops.

How Things Change

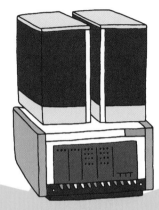

UNIVAC I (1951)

The first computer ever sold, UNIVAC I (UNIVeral Automatic Computer), weighed twice as much as a full-grown African elephant, and required as much power as 250 British homes. It cost over £25 million in modern money. Despite the hefty size and price tag 46 UNIVAC Is were bought, and were used for everything from predicting election results to modelling atomic explosions!

PDP-8 (1965)

The PDP-8 was the first successful 'mini-computer'. 'Mini' here was a relative term: it was small relative to the mainframes like UNIVAC but it was still the size of a wardrobe and cost $18,500 (around £100,000 today). Despite being designed to be as cheap and simple as possible, improvements in technology meant it was 50 times faster than UNIVAC I. PDP-8 was hugely successful, and over 300,000 were sold in a range of models.

IBM 5150 (1981)

Since the early 1960s just about every computer company had tried to develop a 'Personal Computer', or PC, that could fit on a desk, but they were all too big, too complicated, or too expensive. It wasn't until 1981, when IBM released the 5150, that the PC revolution really arrived. The 5150 initially cost at least $1,500 (about £3,000 now), but businesses embraced it, and by 1982 IBM was selling one every single minute. And as its capabilities went up and prices came down, home users began to buy them too, until by 1984 IBM dominated the PC market.

Apple Macintosh 128K (1984)

Apple had been selling PCs since 1976, but they really made their mark in 1984 with the Macintosh 128K. It combined a huge advertising campaign with a novelty that had appeared in only a few minor PCs so far: the Macintosh had a Graphical User Interface, letting less technical people use it. It wasn't long before all PCs had a GUI, though Microsoft's 'Windows' operating system ended up proving more successful than Apple's.

Apple iPhone (2007)

Ever since introducing the Macintosh, Apple had been known for being at the forefront of computer design. In 2007 they revolutionised personal computing with the iPhone, sparking the smartphone revolution, making computing available on a hand-held, always-on device. By 2011 Apple was the most valuable company in the world and people were buying more smartphones than PCs.

Scripting Languages

Programming languages fall into a number of families that share particular ways of working. One of the most popular of these is scripting languages. Scripting languages don't always produce the fastest-running code, but they focus on being quick and compact to write and run, and are usually dynamically typed. This makes them a great set of languages to get started with.

Javascript

Javascript has seen a huge explosion in popularity in recent years. On the surface it's a straightforward scripting language – its syntax is nice and simple, and is shared with a lot of other languages like C++ and Java. The code examples in this book are inspired by Javascript.

What makes Javascript so important is that it is supported by web browsers, so it can be included in web pages. This makes it really easy to get started with Javascript and to share your programs with others. Javascript can also be run outside of browsers like any other scripting language using interpreters like node.js.

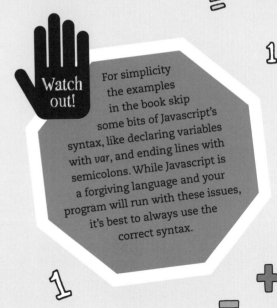

Watch out!

For simplicity the examples in the book skip some bits of Javascript's syntax, like declaring variables with *var*, and ending lines with semicolons. While Javascript is a forgiving language and your program will run with these issues, it's best to always use the correct syntax.

Python

Python is another popular scripting language. It's very easy to develop large programs in, as there are lots of libraries that can easily be added on to provide extra capabilities. It also has a very well-developed class and inheritance model, making it easy to do object-oriented programming.

While Javascript's syntax is shared with many earlier programming languages, Python has its own way of doing lots of things. For instance, rather than curly brackets Python uses indentation (putting spaces before lines) to define code blocks. And while Javascript tends to use things like *for* loops and checking return values for errors, Python code has other ways of solving the same problem, like *iterators* and *exceptions*. So if you do get into Python (and you should – it's a great language), read some tutorials on how to get the most out of its way of doing things.

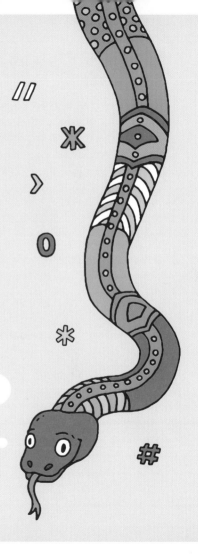

Ahhh, sssssscripting!

Others

There are lots more scripting languages out there too, such as Ruby, Lua, PHP and Perl. Each one has its own strengths and uses, so don't be scared to tackle a new one if it comes along!

More Coding!

Hopefully you enjoyed your first coding experience on page 44. Scratch is an amazing language, and it's a great way to create some simple games and programs. Along with code it's got loads of music and art you can use in your programs, and once you're done you can share them with friends and family! To save programs you'll need to join Scratch and sign in. Then you'll be able to share your code too.

Learning new skills

When you go to the **Create** section of Scratch it will bring up a menu bar on the right with loads of tutorials – these will take you step by step through a range of projects. Whenever you learn a new programming language tutorials are a great way to start, as they're designed to get you familiar with all the things the language can do by showing you exactly how to use them. Go ahead and explore some of Scratch's tutorials.

You can also select **Explore** from the main page to check out games and programs other people have created. Not only can you enjoy the games, but then you can look at the code and see how they were made! Try a few, and then examine the code for your favourite and figure out how it works. You can even change the code and see what effect that has – don't worry about breaking it, your changes won't affect the main version!

Have a go

If you've got a great idea for a program, away you go! If not, here are a couple of ideas:

Code a music program where clicking on different objects plays different notes. Check out the **Sprites** section in the bottom left for a range of objects (a *sprite* is the coding term for a 2D image), the **Sound** menu for music, and the *When a sprite is clicked* Event. Scratch lets you create your own sprites, so why not draw some black and white rectangles and see if you can code up a piano keyboard!

Code a game where a ball bounces around the screen and you get a point every time you click on it. Check out the **Motion** menu for moving and bouncing. You'll also want to create a *score* variable, increase it with each click and make it visible as a scoreboard. Once you've managed that, how about speeding up the ball with each click, or having the game only last for 30 seconds so you and your friends can compete for the highest score?

Setting Code Free

A lot of people around the world make a living from programming – when you buy a videogame some of that money goes to pay the programmers who wrote it. But a lot of coders also write software that they then release online for free.

Some do it as a hobby, some do it as a way to learn programming, and some do it to help people out with useful tools.

Open-source

There's also a special kind of free software, called open-source software. This means that not only can you download the program for free, you can download the program code for it too (called the source code). That means you can read the code to see how the program works, and even modify it yourself!

The idea behind open-source software is that if you like a program you can download the code and change it, making it do new things. Lots of people making small improvements in their spare time can add up to really big programs, like a web browser! You may even have used open-source code without knowing it.

Watch out!

Unfortunately not all programs available online are safe to run. Some might contain viruses that can damage your computer or steal your information! Always check with a parent or teacher before you download any program from the internet.

Getting involved

Big open-source projects can be very complicated, so you should get the hang of a programming language before you dive into them. But once you've got some experience with coding, open-source code can be a great way to see how real programs are made!

Before you start looking at a program, make sure the project still has people actively contributing to it. That way there will be plenty of folks to answer your questions, if you have any.

Making changes

Once you understand how a program works, you can start making changes to it. To get started, try fixing a listed bug. Then other contributors will review your work and tell you if you've made any mistakes, and merge it into the main program.

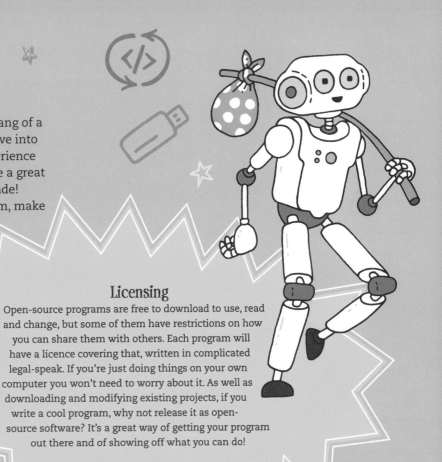

Licensing

Open-source programs are free to download to use, read and change, but some of them have restrictions on how you can share them with others. Each program will have a licence covering that, written in complicated legal-speak. If you're just doing things on your own computer you won't need to worry about it. As well as downloading and modifying existing projects, if you write a cool program, why not release it as open-source software? It's a great way of getting your program out there and of showing off what you can do!

Rise of the Robots

Computer programs don't just control PCs, smartphones and tablets; combine your code with some electronics and you can build yourself a robot! And it's never been easier to get started with this sort of programming, no matter what your level of experience.

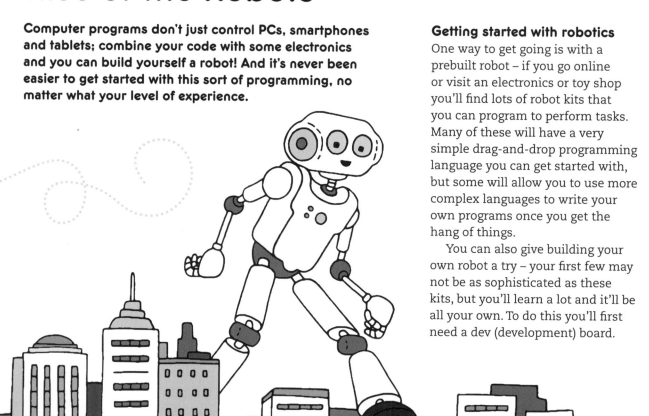

Getting started with robotics

One way to get going is with a prebuilt robot – if you go online or visit an electronics or toy shop you'll find lots of robot kits that you can program to perform tasks. Many of these will have a very simple drag-and-drop programming language you can get started with, but some will allow you to use more complex languages to write your own programs once you get the hang of things.

You can also give building your own robot a try – your first few may not be as sophisticated as these kits, but you'll learn a lot and it'll be all your own. To do this you'll first need a dev (development) board.

This is a little computer you load your programs on to, which can then interact with electronics to control your robot. Some great ways to start are with the BBC micro:bit and the Arduino, though if you already have lots of Lego then you might also want to consider Lego Mindstorms.

Robo-IO

Your dev board will come with a bunch of I/O (Input/Output) pins. You can connect things to these to control them from your dev board. You can start by connecting LEDs and writing programs to make them light up in cool patterns, and even making them spell out messages. Once you understand that, you can start to connect up things like motors and drive your robot around!

As well as your program controlling things, you can also connect up sensors to feed information to your robot. You can get sensors for light, temperature and all sorts of things. Combined with motors you can do things like create a robot that will drive towards the brightest light, and have it chase a torch around the room!

Electricity can be dangerous. Make sure you have an adult check what you're doing to make sure that you won't hurt yourself or damage your kit.

Watch out!

Working with Files

If you want the users of your program to be able to stop and come back to it later, like saving and loading in a computer game, then your program needs to deal with files. Files are places data is kept in your computer's storage. A file can be a photograph, a movie, a text document or any other kind of data.

Filing things away

The syntax for how files are accessed varies a lot between programming languages, but they all share pretty much the same approach. First, you need to *open* the file. This statement takes the path of the file as an argument, such as "C:*my_files**file.txt*", which tells your program which file in particular you want it to open.

The *open* statement will return a file object – this is a representation of the file within your program that you can then read from and write to. Reading means getting data from the file into your program, and writing puts data from your program into the file. The syntax for doing these things is often very similar to how you get input from the keyboard and write it to the screen. Once you've finished using your file, you call the *close* statement on the file object to stop using it.

Restricted access

By default, when you open a file you can read from and write to it, but in many cases you'll only want to do one or the other. In that case it's best to open the file as read-only or write-only. This means your program will only be able to do one of those two things to it. This is particularly handy if you just want to read data from a file – it means you can't accidentally write to it and mess it up!

Filenames generally end in a dot and then a few letters to define what *type* of file this is – this is the file extension. For instance, files containing text end in .txt, while .jpg and .gif are picture formats. You may find your computer hides these by default, in which case you'll need to go online and find out how to make them visible.

Code that Communicates

While the first computers were stand-alone devices, modern computers are usually networked to other computers, allowing them to send and receive data from one another. Data can be transmitted across ethernet cables, or without cables via wireless (Wi-Fi).

Networking in theory

Any data to be sent or received is sent as one or more packets, which are then sent over the wired or wireless link to the nearest switch. This is a physical device that has the job of ensuring these packets end up in the right place by sending them on to their intended destination. As well as your data, each packet starts with a header that describes where it came from and where it is going, so the switch knows where to send it.

This method of pushing packets around is called IP (Internet Protocol). The process of breaking the data you want to send into packets and then putting it back together at the other end is called TCP (Transmission Control Protocol) – this also handles resending any packets that get lost in transmission.

Great to meet you Alan!

Fab to meet you too Geoff! How's tricks?

Networking in practice

All of this sounds (and is!) pretty complicated, but fortunately your computer will take care of it for you. To send or receive data in your program you just create a socket object, which represents the thing you will send/receive data on, just like a file object is how you read and write data.

One difference is that in networking, when you connect to another computer, one side (the server) has to wait for the other side (the client) to make a connection. Just as a laptop has multiple USB ports devices can plug into,

a computer has multiple network ports it can connect with. Unlike the physical ports, though, a computer has *thousands* of network ports available.

In order to make a connection the server program listens on a particular port, while the client program connects by giving the same port, and the address of the server to connect to. Once a connection is established, both sides can send and receive data, rather like writing or reading to a file – instead of *write()* and *read()*, though, you use *send()* and *recv()*.

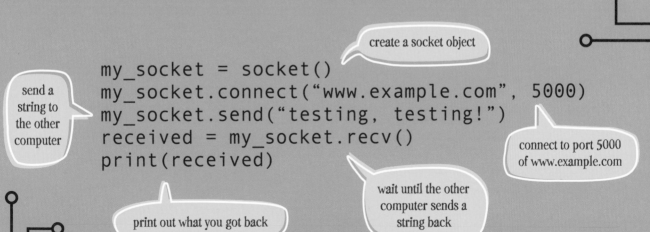

create a socket object

send a string to the other computer

```
my_socket = socket()
my_socket.connect("www.example.com", 5000)
my_socket.send("testing, testing!")
received = my_socket.recv()
print(received)
```

connect to port 5000 of www.example.com

wait until the other computer sends a string back

print out what you got back

Cloudy Weather

The most important trend in computing in recent years has been devices being constantly connected to the internet. Until recently, computer users would only go online when they needed to download something, or look something up. But now, thanks to smartphones and the growth of wireless availability, a lot of computers are online all the time.

That's neat!

The internet was born from a research project in the 1970s between American universities, which created a network of computers named ARPANET. Because ARPANET was designed to survive a nuclear attack it had no central point of control, which is why even today the internet is decentralised, with no person or country in charge of it. In 1989 a British computer scientist named Tim Berners-Lee created the first web page of the World Wide Web, which is how we use the internet.

What is the cloud?

Devices that are always online can use a new technique: cloud computing. This essentially means that tasks a computer would once handle locally, such as storing files and performing computation, can now be offloaded to computers on the internet. Because it doesn't matter where in the world these computers are, they're said to be a 'cloud'.

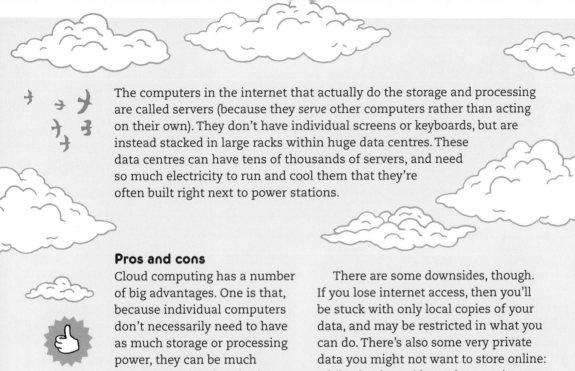

The computers in the internet that actually do the storage and processing are called servers (because they *serve* other computers rather than acting on their own). They don't have individual screens or keyboards, but are instead stacked in large racks within huge data centres. These data centres can have tens of thousands of servers, and need so much electricity to run and cool them that they're often built right next to power stations.

Pros and cons

Cloud computing has a number of big advantages. One is that, because individual computers don't necessarily need to have as much storage or processing power, they can be much cheaper. Storing data in the cloud also means that if you lose or break your computer all your data is still safe and can be loaded onto a replacement. And you can easily access the same data from any desktop, laptop or smartphone.

There are some downsides, though. If you lose internet access, then you'll be stuck with only local copies of your data, and may be restricted in what you can do. There's also some very private data you might not want to store online: while cloud providers take security very seriously, there have been a number of occasions when hackers have been able to steal information from data centres.

Waiting In Line

We've already explored _arrays_, which are a way of storing data in a block of memory, with every individual piece of data accessible at any time. Not all data is suited to being stored this way, though.

Linking up

Another way to store data is in a linked list. Here, rather than storing all the data in a single big block of memory like an array, each piece of data is stored separately, and contains a link to the next element in the list, like links in a chain. So item A has a link to item B, which has a link to item C. A singly linked list only has links in this direction, while a doubly linked list has links in both directions (C links back to B, which links back to A).

In order to access an item from a linked list you need to iterate through the list, following the links in the chain. This is slower than an array, where any item in the middle can be reached in one operation. But it's easy to add and remove links from a list, whereas – because they are a single block of memory – arrays are harder to shrink or grow.

Queuing and stacking

Arrays and linked lists are used to implement certain types of storage that the computer relies upon internally: queues and stacks. These are data stores where, rather than being able to access any element, you can only read one element at a time, based on the order in which the elements were put in.

A queue operates by FIFO – First In, First Out. So if you add A, then B, to a queue, when you read from the queue you will get first A, then B. In contrast, a stack operates by LIFO – Last In, First Out. Here if you add A, then B, to a stack, then when you read from it you will first get B, then A, rather like putting things onto and taking things off a *stack* of paper.

Don't push it!

That's neat!
Putting an item into a stack is referred to as pushing it, whereas taking one out is called popping it!

Last in, first out.

87

Playing Games

Since the first computer was built, programmers have been working out how to use them to play games! Pong, a black-and-white tennis game that involved two white rectangles for rackets and a square for the ball, came out in 1972 as a coin-operated arcade game, and by 1974 was available for home users.

These days the biggest video games, called AAA or triple-A games, require teams of hundreds of programmers, artists and testers to work for years, and can cost more than £100 million to develop. They feature cutting-edge 3D graphics and often push computers to the very limit of their capabilities.

Indie gaming

However, these aren't the only games out there. Recent advances in the tools available to coders has led to an explosion of indie games, produced by single programmers or small teams, often working in their spare time. The ease with which these games can be developed means that coders can experiment with gameplay and create amazing new types of game. Minecraft, perhaps the biggest computer game in the world, was created by a single programmer as a hobby project!

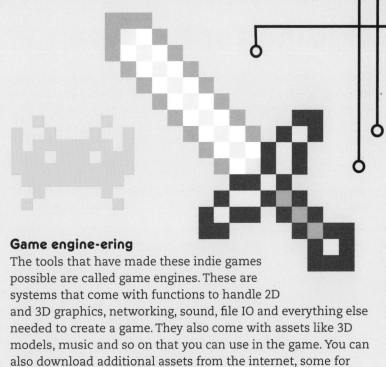

Smartphones and tablets have also provided another great way for individuals to develop games; they lend themselves well to small, simple games that a single person or small team can develop. Their app stores make it easy to distribute games, and for people to potentially even make some money from games they develop as a hobby.

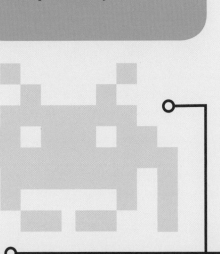

Game engine-ering

The tools that have made these indie games possible are called game engines. These are systems that come with functions to handle 2D and 3D graphics, networking, sound, file IO and everything else needed to create a game. They also come with assets like 3D models, music and so on that you can use in the game. You can also download additional assets from the internet, some for free, and some in exchange for money.

To make a game you then need to write your own code to tell the engine what to do in every circumstance. Each engine has different commands, and will support different programming languages – some are very easy to use, while others are more complicated and powerful. Some are for developing games for PCs, some for the web, and some for smartphones.

Coding for the Internet

Creating websites is a fantastic way to get started with computing – who wouldn't love to have their own website? There's tons of help available online, and you don't need any additional software installed on your PC – if you have a web browser and a text editor you can get started!

Web pages are written in a syntax called HTML. They contain the words that go on the page, along with the addresses of images you want to include, links and any other content. You can also include formatting (colours, sizes, alignment and everything else that describes precisely how your content looks) directly in the file, or in a separate CSS (Cascading Style Sheet) file.

Getting dynamic

If you want your web pages to really come alive you can embed computer code directly into your page! Browsers support Javascript, which you can write directly into the HTML file or include as a separate .js file. Then whenever someone loads your web page your code will run right in their browser.

The code you write will be triggered by callbacks. The browser provides lots of callbacks you can use, so you can write code that runs . . .

- when the page loads
- when someone presses a button
- when someone types in a text box

. . . and in lots of other ways.

Your code can then make changes to the web page. That could be anything from resizing some text to completely changing the entire page! Within the Javascript code the web page is represented by the DOM (Document Object Model) – much like with a socket or file object, this is a representation of the web page within your code. Whatever you do to the DOM will appear on the page.

For security reasons there are some things you can't do within the browser. However, it's a powerful and flexible language, and a recent update to web pages called HTML5 has added even more capabilities, such as a *canvas* element you can use to put dynamic drawings and animations directly into web pages.

From now on, whenever you browse the web and notice a page doing something particularly cool, be aware that it's using Javascript someone wrote to do it. Think about *how* it's doing it, and maybe see if you can figure out how to do it yourself!

Cool!

Making Things Smart

It's not just PCs and smartphones that are always online. Wireless technology is now small and cheap enough that it can be built into all sorts of devices, along with the sensors and microchips needed to control it. That means that you can now get thermostats, speakers and even light bulbs that report their status and receive commands over the internet, making them smart.

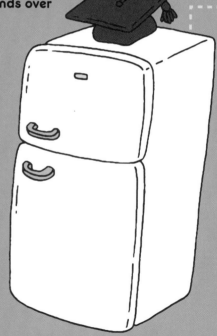

It may not be long before just about everything electrical in your house will be connected to the wireless network, sharing data and being controllable from your smartphone or PC. You could have music follow you from room to room, turn off your heating if you're not around, and have more control over your personal electronics than ever before. This vision of a world of smart devices is called the Internet of Things.

Taking control

As a programmer, though, you can get even more out of the Internet of Things. As well as having smartphone apps, many of these smart devices can be controlled via APIs, which means you can write code to control them yourselves. An API, or application programming interface, is a set of network commands that the device will listen for, along with documentation to tell you what they are and how to use them.

Smartening up

As well as controlling other devices, if you are creating your own electronic devices, like a robot, then why not make it controllable via wireless? That way, rather than having to load new code onto it every time you make a change, you can write the control code on your PC, and have it control your robot over the network. Some development boards like the Raspberry Pi have networking built in, while others like the Arduino have add-ons for it, and there are libraries for each that make it easy to hook your robot up to your wireless network.

That's neat!

While you could write network and API code yourself, you will usually be able to find a software library for your programming language that does that for you, so you just need to worry about what you want the device to do. When possible you should make use of third-party libraries like this, rather than try to write everything yourself. It will save you a lot of time, and with lots of people using the same code and reporting any issues, these libraries can be made as good as possible.

Keeping Track of Code

Programs are just text files, but we've already seen how smart editors and IDEs can make writing code quicker and easier. In the same way, while you can just save your programs to disk, version control makes it easier to save and load versions of your code.

Version control is a way of keeping track of the changes you make to a file. To use it, you first create a repository, which will store one or more programs. You then write your program as normal, except periodically, when you're happy with the state it's in, you commit the code to the repository.

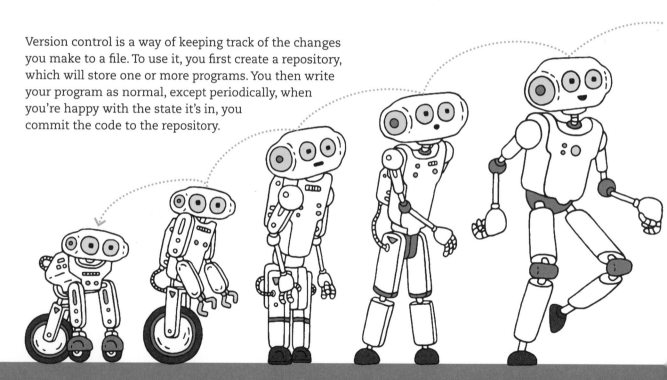

Going back in time

The version control system contains a history of each set of changes you've made. If you find you've made some mistakes and broken your code and don't know how to fix it, you can revert to an earlier version. You can also see precisely what changes you made over time in the form of diffs, which show what changed between each commit of code.

Your version control system can be purely local to your machine, but there are also free online version control systems such as GitHub. These have two big advantages. Because they're a *cloud service*, you can work on your code from multiple machines, and recover it if one breaks. They also make it really easy for you to share your code with other people, as the repositories are public (viewable by anyone) by default.

Working with others

Indeed, sharing code is where the real value of version control comes in – it's the best way for multiple people to work on the same code. It keeps track of everyone's changes and will help them resolve any conflicts. Modern version control systems are distributed, which means everyone has a local copy of the repository. They get changes from the master repository by pulling from it, and push their local commits to it.

Version control systems are how open-source projects are coordinated. Rather than pushing code commits directly into the repository, commits are filed as pull requests. People who know the code well then review the requests and either accept them into the main program, or return it with comments about what needs fixing. This means that if you contribute to a big project, someone will review your code and help you make it as good as possible.

Getting Old-school

The scripting languages we've looked at, such as Python and Javascript, aren't the only family of programming languages that are widely used. Now we'll look at some lower-level languages that are used to write a lot of the programs that run on PCs every day.

C and C++

Of these, C and C++ are very important. C is a venerable language that dates back to the early 1970s, while C++ is an updated version that includes classes and a host of other advancements. C++ is a more demanding, slower language to code in than most scripting languages, with lots of powerful techniques, such as direct access to the computer's memory through pointers.

C++ and other languages of its type can't be run directly; they must first be compiled. This is a process where the programmer must first convert their program to machine code using a compiler program. It's this executable that is then distributed to users. This means that different operating systems need different compilers and different executables (because their machine code is different).

However, this compilation step does mean many problems can be found at compile time rather than when the program runs. It also generally means the code runs faster, because it's already been translated into something the computer can run directly. Because of this speed, and the language's long history, there's a lot of software out there written in C and C++, including most computer operating systems.

Java

C and C++ aren't the only languages with lots of pre-existing software – Java is another. This is a newer language, developed in the 1990s. It's inspired by C++ but designed to be easier to write and more portable. Unlike C++, Java takes care of a lot of memory management, and makes it very easy to add libraries of functionality.

Most importantly, Java's not compiled directly to machine code. Instead it's turned into bytecode, which can then be run on any operating system through an interpreter. As such it's halfway between a compiled language and a scripting language, and there's no need to recompile it for different operating systems – a Java program can run anywhere.

Java is used for a lot of software that manages websites and servers. While it and C++ aren't the best languages to get started with, if you get interested in open-source development you'll find a lot of code written in these languages.

I may be old but I still function!

Working in Parallel

All the programs you've seen so far involve the computer following instructions one at a time. Given how fast computers are, this is usually just fine. But sometimes you'll need bits of your program to operate independently at the same time, and that's where parallelism comes in.

Branching out

Parallelism means running more than one piece of your program at the same time, in parallel. Rather like the limbs of a tree that split into lots of branches as it grows, your program can fork into multiple branches too. Each of these branches are called threads or processes. Each one is essentially its own separate and independent program, executing instructions one at a time.

So why run things in parallel? It's so you can do things that may take a long time, without holding up other bits of program. For instance, the GUI (see page 54) of a program is often run separately from the rest of the program. That way even if the main part of your program takes a long time

calculating something, the user can still scroll around and click buttons, as the GUI code is running independently.

Your code branches will need to communicate, though: when your user presses a button in the GUI, you want something to happen in your main program. Programming languages have different ways to do this. Often they will use queues to pass messages between branches – one branch writes a message that the other branch then reads when it's free.

Locking and unlocking

Writing parallel code (sometimes called multi-threaded code) can get complicated. For instance, different branches can share the same variable, but big problems can occur if more than one tries to use it at the same time. To avoid this there are various types of locks (such as mutexes and semaphores) that ensure only one branch accesses a variable at a time. If another wants to use it too, it has to wait until the first branch is done and removes the lock.

That's neat!

Computers can actually do more than one thing at a time – modern computers have CPUs with two, four, or more cores, each of which can run a thread or process. However, you can have far more processes than that – the CPU switches between the processes really, really quickly, so it seems like everything's running at once!

Hold it, hold it. Now go, go, GO!

Supercomputing

Back when computers were first invented they took up an entire room, but now a computer fits under a desk or in the palm of your hand. And yet there are still computers that take up whole buildings: these are the supercomputers.

That's neat!

As well as the weather, supercomputers have long been used to design and simulate the most destructive weapons in existence: atomic bombs. While that may not seem particularly appealing, it made various Test Ban treaties possible. The various countries with atomic weapons agreed they would no longer try them out them in the real world any more, but would instead simulate them using supercomputers.

Up, up and away!

Supercomputers are incredibly powerful machines that are used to solve mind-bogglingly complicated problems. The most common are simulating very complex real-world systems, such as weather patterns (so we can predict when it will rain), or how protein molecules fold up (to find new medical cures).

Since there's a limit to how large a single CPU (see page 52) can be, supercomputers are actually made up of thousands of individual CPUs connected together. The programs that run on them are written to be massively *parallel*: the calculations are split up into thousands of tasks which are then distributed to the individual CPUs.

Rent your own supercomputer

Supercomputers cost many millions of pounds, which obviously puts them out of reach of pretty much everyone. And yet, with the advent of *cloud computing*, it's now possible to rent computing time by the minute. So a scientist who needs a supercomputer to solve a particular problem can simply rent as much computing power as she needs for an hour or so to run her program, getting temporary access to her own supercomputer for just a few hundred pounds.

Getting into the Algo-rhythm

Computers do things fast – a computer that costs £5 can have a clock speed of 1GHz, meaning it does one *billion* things every second. So most of the time you won't need to worry about how quickly your program runs. Sometimes, though, you may find a program takes a long time to complete. That's when you need to worry about the algorithms you are using.

An algorithm is just the way your code is solving a particular task – such as sorting a list into alphabetical order. There's usually lots of ways to write code to complete a task, and each has its own complexity – that's how the time it takes to run changes as you increase the amount of data.

How complex is your code?

An algorithm with complexity $O(n)$ is called linear – that means if you double the size of your data set (n) it takes twice as long to run. But another algorithm for the same task might have complexity $O(n^2)$ – now when you double the amount of data the algorithm takes *four* times as long to run. When n is small the time differences don't matter, but if you're working with millions of elements the second algorithm can take tens of thousands of times longer than the first to solve the same task!

There are lots of other possible complexities – the smaller the value inside the bracket comes to for a value of n, the faster the algorithm will run on large sets of data. To work out the complexity of your own algorithms take a look at the code and try to work out how many times it will need to run for n pieces of data. Nested loops (loops inside other loops) are a sign that your algorithm may have a high complexity. Consider if there's a way to rewrite it to avoid these if you're planning to deal with lots of data.

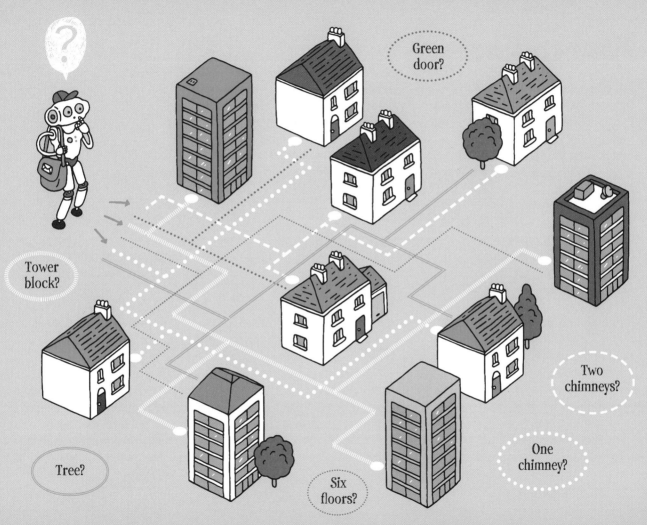

Faster, Faster!

You may have noticed that every year computers get better – the same amount of money will buy a faster CPU, more memory, and more storage.

This has actually been going on for a long time. Back in 1965 Gordon Moore, one of the founders of Intel (still one of the world's biggest CPU manufacturers to this day), noticed that the number of transistors they could fit into the same amount of silicon doubled every year – essentially making the same size CPU twice as powerful.

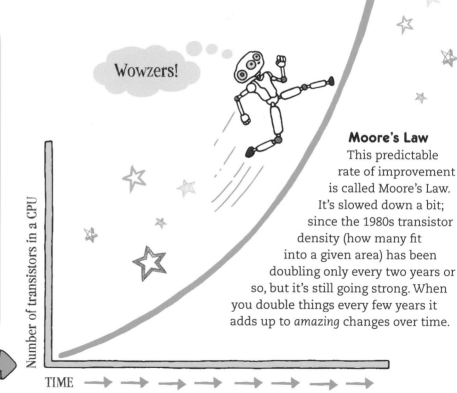

Wowzers!

Number of transistors in a CPU

TIME

Moore's Law
This predictable rate of improvement is called Moore's Law. It's slowed down a bit; since the 1980s transistor density (how many fit into a given area) has been doubling only every two years or so, but it's still going strong. When you double things every few years it adds up to *amazing* changes over time.

Really big and really small numbers

This advancement has been driven by manufacturers managing to make their transistors ever smaller. The vacuum tubes used in Colossus and ENIAC were each several centimetres wide. In contrast, the silicon transistors in modern CPUs are just 14 *nanometres* (0.000000014m) across. The first CPU chips from the 1970s had a few thousand transistors, while modern ones have over a *billion*.

Modern transistors are actually so small that many scientists think Moore's Law will have to give out soon; 14-nanometre transistors are fewer than 100 individual atoms across, and if they get much smaller then weird quantum effects will start to disrupt them. However, scientists are experimenting with new materials, 3D arrangements of transistors, and anything else they can think of to try and keep Moore's Law on track. Who knows how long they'll be able to keep it up?

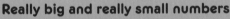

Coding for Phones and Tablets

The release of the first iPhone created a new type of programming: app development. Smartphone and tablet apps can be a great way to get into coding since there's lots of support for creating and distributing them, and you can make fun apps and games you can easily share with your friends.

Kitting yourself out

To develop a phone or tablet app you need a Software Development Kit, or SDK. Android and iOS (iPhone/iPad) have their own SDKs, as do other phone types like Windows. An app you write using the Android SDK will work on any Android device, but not an iPhone, and vice versa.

SDKs can be downloaded for free and come with everything you need to develop an app. Along with an IDE (see page 41) for the programming language the device supports, they include APIs (see page 93) to access things like the camera or speakers on the device, a GUI framework (see page 54), and even a simulator that will let you try your app on a simulated phone or tablet.

Once you're happy with your app you'll be able to run it on a real device! The SDK has ways to upload it to your personal phone so you can see how it works for real, and share it with friends and family. The ultimate step is to upload it to the app store, where you can even charge money for it. Getting an app into the app store involves jumping through a lot of hoops, though!

A choice of languages

Each SDK has its own APIs and programming language; Android uses Java, while iOS uses Swift or Objective-C. Learning to use an SDK can be a bit intimidating, with new languages and APIs. But the SDKs include tutorials that will walk you through just about anything you want to do.

One alternative to developing apps using SDKs (called native apps because they use the native language and APIs of the device) is to develop web apps instead. This means writing apps using Javascript, CSS and HTML5. At its simplest this means just developing web pages that work well with smartphones and tablets. But there are also SDKs that let you create apps using these web techniques, rather than the native languages of the device.

Even More Coding

Hopefully this book has got you all fired up and ready to get coding. Here are some great places to get started! Teachers, friends and family may also be able to point you at even more.

Getting started

- **Scratch** www.scratch.mit.edu is a site you've already explored on pages 44 and 74. Click on Explore at the very top and check out all the amazing things people have made with it – can you make something like that?
- **Code tutorials** There are hundreds of sites out there that will get you started in a variety of programming languages, and www.codecademy.com is one of the best. You can also check out www.freecodecamp.com for another great tutorial site, with a focus on open-source development.
- **Search** It may sound odd, but www.google.com and other search engines are your best friend when learning to code. If you have an error message you don't understand, copy it into your search engine and you'll find loads of web pages explaining what it means.

Coding tools

- **Smart editors** If you use Windows, try www.notepad-plus-plus.org for a nice and simple smart text editor. If you're a Mac user, try www.macromates.com.
- **Fiddles** If you want to jump right into coding without installing anything, www.pythonfiddle.com will let you test out small Python programs right in your browser. www.jsfiddle.net does the same for Javascript, and lets you easily combine it with HTML and CSS.
- **iOS and Android SDKs** If you're looking to develop phone apps you can download the iOS SDK from https://developer.apple.com/ios to develop iPhone/iPad apps. Head to https://developer.android.com/studio for the Android equivalent.
- **Web app** If you want to write phone apps in Javascript instead, check out www.ionicframework.com for an SDK that will let you write apps using web code.
- **Version control** There are lots of version control systems out there, but www.github.com is by far the most popular – as well as storing your own code, it's where most open-source programs are kept.

> Come on,
> let's do this!

Creating games

- **Web games** If you want to get started creating games, check out www.scirra.com/construct2, where you build games in HTML5 using the simple programming language built into the engine. If you want more control try www.phaser.io, which lets you use Javascript to directly control your web game.
- **Unity** If you want to create 3D games, head to www.unity3d.com for a powerful engine used to develop lots of commercial games. It can be a bit overwhelming, but with it you can create amazing 2D and 3D games for just about any platform there is!

Getting physical

- **BBC micro:bit** One of the easiest ways to start programming physical devices is with the BBC micro:bit. Your school may be able to provide you with one, and www.microbit.org allows you to program it very simply in a range of languages. There's even a simulator on the website you can use to test your program!
- **Other dev boards** The next step up, complexity-wise, is an Arduino (www.arduino.cc). It's primarily programmed in C, but there's lots of help available. It also has a fantastic range of add-on devices to expand its capabilities. If you want even more power try the Raspberry Pi (www.raspberrypi.org). This is a tiny PC you can do just about anything with!
- **Mindstorms** If you're a fan of Lego, check out Lego Mindstorms (www.lego.com/en-gb/mindstorms). You can use this to turn your Lego creations into robots you can program with a simple drag-and-drop language.

Coding Glossary

Argument A variable that is passed into a function to change how it operates.

Array An object that can store lots of individual values, any of which can be accessed via square brackets (such as arr[5]).

Binary A way of counting that only uses 1s and 0s.

Bit A single 1 or 0 value that represents how data is actually stored in a computer's memory.

Boolean A value used in logic that can either be True or False.

Bug A mistake that causes a program not to run, or to do the wrong thing when it does run.

Byte A collection of 8 bits that can be accessed together, and can be used to store a single character.

Callback A function whose name is passed as an argument, letting other code call back to it. Often used in GUIs.

Class An object that can be used to store all the variables and functions related to a particular task or thing.

Comment Text that can be added to programs to remind yourself or others what that particular part of the code is doing.

Comparison operator A range of operators such as equal to, less than and greater than that let programs compare two values and make a decision based on logic.

CPU The tiny chip inside all computers that carries out the instructions in every program.

Data centre A place containing lots of servers that can provide data over the internet.

Else The alternative to If, defining what to do if an If condition wasn't True. Can be combined with If to form a new conditional, Else If.

File Information such as a photo, video or text that is stored on a computer.

Floating point A number with a decimal place, such as 1.381, -21.9 or 8.0.

For loop Type of loop that runs for a certain number of times.

Function A block of code that has been separated out and that can be called from elsewhere in the program.

Graphical User Interface (GUI) A way of letting people use a program via pictures and buttons rather than just typing.

If Part of a program that only runs if a particular condition is True.

Instruction A piece of code that tells the computer to do something.

Integer A whole number (no decimal places) that can be positive, negative or 0.

Javascript A programming language that can be included in web pages to run when someone reads the page.

Linked list An alternative to arrays when storing lots of values, with each element linking to the next element in the list.

Logic Allows programs to make decisions based on whether values in the program are True or False.

Loop Part of a program that runs over and over again until a particular condition is met.

Machine code A set of instructions the CPU can understand and follow. Programming languages are turned into machine code before they run.

Memory Where variables and other data needed by a program are kept. Unlike storage, memory is volatile, meaning that when the computer turns off it is forgotten.

Networking The ability for computers to communicate with one another, either via wires or wirelessly using electromagnetic waves.

Open source Programs that people have shared on the internet so that you can download, use and even make changes to them.

Program A list of instructions that the computer follows from top to bottom, carrying out each one as it comes to it.

Programming language The way code can tell the computer to do things. Different programming languages write code in different ways.

Python A powerful but easy-to-learn programming language that has its own syntax and way of doing things.

Queue A way of storing data where elements can only be read from the queue in the order they are put into it.

Refactoring Rewriting code, not to change what it does, but to make it neater or faster.

Return A value returned to the calling code when a function ends.

Scratch A visual programming language that allows you to drag and drop code elements rather than needing to write the program out.

Server A computer without a monitor or other controls that serves other computers by providing them with data over a network.

Stack A way of storing data where the only element that can be read is the one added to the stack most recently.

Static typing Programming languages that only allow a variable to ever contain one type of value (like Boolean or integer), making certain errors easy to catch.

Storage Where files and data are kept. Storage is slower to access than memory, but data in storage is remembered even when the computer is switched off.

String A word or phrase in quote marks (such as 'Hello, world').

Transistor An incredibly tiny switch. A CPU contains billions of transistors, and by turning on and off they carry out all of the operations inside the computer.

Type What kind of data a variable is storing, such as a string, integer or Boolean.

Variable A named place to store a piece of data, such as a number or word, which can then be used later in the program.

While loop A type of loop that continues to run while a certain condition is True.

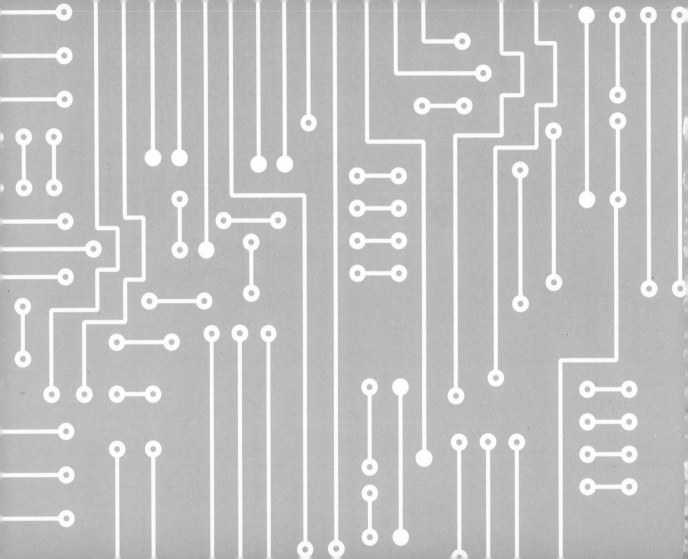